CHURCH HISTORY

CHURCH HISTORY

An Essential Guide

Justo L. González

ABINGDON PRESS
Nashville

CHURCH HISTORY:
AN ESSENTIAL GUIDE

This book is printed on acid-free, recycled paper.

Library of Congress Cataloging-in-Publication Data

González, Justo L.
Church history: an essential guide
p. cm.
Includes bibliographical references
ISBN 0-687-01611-8 (alk. paper)
1. Church history. I. Title.
BR145.2.G65
270—dc20 96-20588
CIP

ISBN 13: 978-0-687-01611-2

11 12 13 14 15 16 17 - 27 26 25 24 23 22 21

MANUFACTURED IN THE UNITED STATES OF AMERICA

Contents

Introduction

The Purpose of this Book

This book was born out of the experience of many years in the teaching of church history. I have come to the conclusion that one of the main difficulties for beginning students in the field is the lack of a global vision of church history. Many do not know whether the Crusades took place before the Reformation or after. Therefore, as they move into a course on church history, they feel as if entering a dark cave that leads them ever deeper into unknown territory, without having any idea what there might be beyond the next turn.

In such circumstances, it becomes difficult for students to distinguish between that which is fundamental and that which is secondary, with the sad result that some spend hours memorizing details, and never achieve a global vision of what was taking place at a particular time, or how this has impacted the later history of the church.

This book is an attempt to respond to that need. It does not aspire to be a traditional textbook for the field, since it lacks detail and nuancing. Rather, it hopes to be a map, or a bird's-eye view, so that a student taking a first voyage through history will not have to do so without a guide or compass. One who is afraid of losing the way can hardly enjoy the scenery. And, since I am in love with the territory, I wish to make it possible for my readers and students to enjoy the scenery!

On the other hand, an abbreviated history is like a fleshless skeleton: even though it may give us an idea of the basic structure of the body, it tells us little of what the person was in real life. Therefore, I urge my readers to use this book, not as a way to know the outlines of the history of the church without actually studying that history, but rather as a map so that they may really move into the fascinating study of this history, which is no less than the life, the disappointments, and the hopes of those who went before us in the faith. By making serious use of the suggestions for further reading as a first clue for more detailed study of subjects which here are barely mentioned, the reader's efforts will be amply rewarded.

The Structure of this Book

What follows includes an *Overview* and nine chapters. The *Overview* briefly tells the entire course of the history of Christianity. By reading it, you will have a complete, although very sketchy, understanding of the order of the main events, and how they relate among themselves.

In that *Overview*, all of church history is divided into nine periods. As with any such attempt, this division is somewhat arbitrary, and has been chosen partly for pedagogical convenience and partly for other reasons. In the rest of the book each chapter corresponds to one of the periods described in the *Overview*.

Furthermore, in each of those nine chapters almost all that is said in the *Overview* is repeated. These quotes are in *italics*, and they serve as an outline to the chapter itself. Thus, in reading those chapters, you may easily go back to the *Overview* in order to see where you are in the entire outline, and how what you are reading relates to what you have read or are about to read.

Following the suggestions of a colleague who read this book in its initial stages, I seriously considered the possibility of including a glossary of new or difficult terms. However, as I sought to do that I became convinced that to produce such a glossary in a really helpful way would result in a much larger book than I had intended. Since all that is said in the *Overview* is amplified in later chapters, many of the unfamiliar words used there will be explained in those other chapters. Therefore, if in reading the *Overview* there is something that is not completely clear, the best procedure is to read what is said about it in the corresponding chapter. Also, when in those chapters the name of a movement or doctrine is mentioned with no further explanation, the suggested readings will help you learn more about it.

Suggested Readings

At the end of each chapter, you will find a list of "suggested readings" from the general surveys of church history most commonly used in colleges, universities, and seminaries in the United States. Since this book is no more than an outline, it is suggested that you choose at least one of those general surveys and use it to amplify what is said here. Again, this book should not be used as a substitute for those fuller surveys, but rather as a guide to them. Thus, as you read each chapter you may wish to go back to the *Overview* in order to see how what you are reading fits into the rest of the history of Christianity, and then to read some of the suggested readings in order to understand more fully the events described in that chapter, and the issues raised in a particular period.

I trust that these instructions are sufficiently clear. If not, the best way to learn is by practice. Therefore, dear reader, launch into the reading of this book and through it into that fascinating adventure which is the history of Christianity!

Overview

The study of history is usually divided into periods. Such division is useful, since it helps to highlight the changes that have taken place from one time to another, and to order our knowledge within a framework. It is important to understand, however, that such divisions are always somewhat artificial, and that therefore it is possible to divide the same history in different ways.

Keeping that in mind, the history to be outlined here may be divided in the following periods, each to be discussed in a separate chapter in this book.

1. The Ancient Church

From the Beginnings of Christianity until Constantine Put an End to Persecution (Edict of Milan, Year 313)

This was a formative period that set the tone for the entire history of the church, for even today we live under the influence of some of the decisions made at that time.

Christianity was born in a world that already had its own religions, cultures, and social and political structures. Within that framework, the new faith made its way, while at the same time defining itself.

The first and most important task of early Christianity was to define its own nature vis-à-vis the Jewish tradition in which it was born. As may be seen in the New Testament, a significant context for that process of definition was the mission to the Gentiles.

Soon Christianity had its first conflicts with the state, and it was within that context that the new faith had to determine its relationship with the surrounding culture, as well as with the political and social institutions that both expressed and supported that culture.

Those conflicts with the state produced both martyrs and "apologists." The first sealed their witness with their blood. The apologists sought to defend the Christian faith in the face of the various accusations made against it. (And some, such as Justin, were first apologists and eventually martyrs.) This attempt to defend the faith produced some of the earliest theological works of Christianity.

But there were other challenges to faith, which most Christians eventually called "heresies"—that is, doctrines which seemed to threaten the very core of the Christian message. It was in response to such heresies that the early church produced the canon (or list of books) of the New Testament, the creed that is usually called "the Apostles' Creed," and the doctrine of apostolic succession.

After the apologists came the first great teachers of the faith —people such as Irenaeus, Tertullian, Clement of Alexandria, Origen, and Cyprian. They wrote works whose impact is felt to this day.

Finally, it is important to point out that, in spite of the scarcity of documents describing it, it is possible to know something about the daily life and the worship of Christians during those first years.

2. The Christian Empire

From the Edict of Milan (313) to the Fall of the Last Roman Emperor of the West (476)

With the "conversion" of the Emperor Constantine, things changed radically. The persecuted church became first the tolerated church, and eventually the official religion of the Roman Empire. In consequence the church, which until then was composed mostly of people from the lower echelons of society, made headway among the aristocracy.

The change was not easy, and Christians responded in many different ways. Some were so grateful for the new situation that it was difficult for them to take a critical stance before the government and society. Others fled to the desert or to remote places and took up the monastic life. Still others simply broke away from the majority church, insisting that they were the true church. There was also a pagan reaction of people seeking to re-establish the ancient religion and its relationship with the state.

The most outstanding leaders of Christianity took a middle position: they continued living in the cities and taking part of the life of society, but with a critical stance. It was thus that, finally freed from the constant threat of persecution, the church produced some of its greatest teachers. It was a time in which great theological treatises were produced, as well as important works of spirituality, and the first history of the church. But it was also a time of bitter theological controversies— especially the one that had to do with Arianism and Trinitarian doctrine.

This period came to an end with the invasions of the "barbarians," Germanic peoples who broke into the Roman Empire and settled in its territories. In the year 410, the Goths took and sacked Rome itself, and in 476 the last Western emperor (Romulus Augustus) was deposed.

3. The Early Middle Ages

From the Fall of Romulus Augustus (476)
to the Schism between East and West (1054)

Since the Roman Empire had earlier been divided into two main regions (the Western Empire, where Latin was spoken, and the Eastern, where Greek was spoken), the invasions of the "barbarians" did not affect all of Christendom in the same way. They had a much deeper impact on the Latin-speaking Western church than on the Eastern and Greek-speaking branch of Christianity.

In the Latin West (what today is Spain, France, Italy, etc.) there was a period of chaos. The Empire ceased to exist, and its place was taken by a number of barbarian kingdoms. Since these were times of pain, death, and disorder, Christian worship, instead of centering on the victory of the Lord and on his resurrection, began to be concerned more and more with death, sin, and repentance. Therefore communion, which until then had been a celebration, became a funereal service, in which one was to think more on one's own sins than on the victory of the Lord.

Much of the ancient culture disappeared, and the only institution that preserved some of it was the church. For that reason, even in the midst of chaos, the church became ever stronger and more influential, with monasticism and the papacy playing important roles in the process.

Meanwhile in the East, the Roman Empire (now called also the Byzantine Empire) continued for another thousand years. There the state was much more powerful than the church, and the former frequently imposed its will on the latter. There were also in that area important theological controversies that helped clarify Christological doctrine. One of the results of these controversies was a number of dissident or independent churches that continue to this day —churches that usually go by the designations "Nestorian" and "Monophysite."

Toward the middle of this period Islam arose as a new threat to the church. It soon conquered vast territories and cities that until then had been important centers in the life of the church— Jerusalem, Antioch, Alexandria, Carthage, etc.

At the same time that Islam was experiencing its greatest territorial expansion, in western Europe a new political power was growing in the Kingdom of the Franks, whose most powerful ruler was Charlemagne. In the year 800 the Pope crowned Charlemagne "emperor," in an attempt to resurrect the ancient Western Roman Empire. Although the new empire was never the same as the old, the title (and sometimes the power) continued to exist for centuries.

The result was that Christianity, which until that time had existed mainly around an axis running from east to west across the Mediterranean, now began to revolve around a new line running from north to south, from the kingdom of the Franks to Rome. However, although here in the West the church seemed to be quite powerful, the truth was that it had difficulty trying to stem the surrounding chaos—and that to a degree the strife within the church itself contributed to the chaos. The measure of order that was achieved took the form of "feudalism," in which each feudal lord followed his own policies, making war as he pleased, and sometimes even falling into brigandage.

It was in the East that there was still a certain degree of order, and where the literature and the knowledge of antiquity were best preserved. But Constantinople, the ancient capital of the Byzantine Empire, was progressively losing its influence. Probably the greatest achievement of Byzantine Christianity was the conversion of Russia, usually dated on the year 988. The relation between the East and the West became increasingly tense, until the definitive rupture in 1054.

4. The High Point of the Middle Ages

From the Schism Between East and West (1054) to the Beginning of the Decline of the Papacy (1303)

The Western church stood in need of a radical reformation, and this came from among the ranks of monasticism. Eventually those monastics who longed for a reformation came to take hold of the papacy, which gave rise to a series of reformist popes. This however led to conflict between the secular and the ecclesiastical authorities, and particularly between popes and emperors.

This was the time of the Crusades, which began in 1095 and lasted for several centuries. And it was also the time of the Spanish "Reconquista"—the process by which the Moors were expelled from the Iberian Peninsula.

In part as a result of the Crusades, commerce flourished, and in consequence the cities also grew, for they themselves were centers of trade. Money, which had practically disappeared during the earlier period, began to circulate again. These events gave rise to a new class, the "bourgeoisie" (that is, people from the city), who lived by trade and later through the development of industry.

As a response to the new conditions, several new monastic orders arose. Most important among them were the Franciscans and Dominicans, known as mendicant orders for their practice of supporting themselves through begging. They produced a new awakening in missionary work, and also penetrated the universities, where they became the leaders in the theology of the time—a theology called "scholastic." That theology reached its high point in Bonaventure (a Franciscan) and Thomas Aquinas (a Dominican).

The growth of cities also gave rise to the great cathedrals. The "romanesque" style that had dominated ecclesiastical architecture in the earlier period now ceded its place to "gothic," which produced the most impressive cathedrals of all times.

Finally, it was also during this period that the papacy reached the height of its prestige and power, in the person of Innocent III (1198-1216). But already toward the end of this period, in the year 1303, the papacy had begun its decline.

5. The Late Middle Ages

From the First Signs of Decline in the Papacy (1303) to the Fall of Constantinople (1453)

The growing bourgeoisie became an ally of the monarchy in each country, and this brought an end to feudalism and produced the beginning of modern nations. But nationalism itself soon became an obstacle to the unity of the church. During a significant part of this period, France and England were at war (the "Hundred Years' War"), and most of the rest of Europe also became involved in the conflict. It was also the time of the "plague," which decimated the population of Europe and produced great demographic and economic upheaval.

The decline of the papacy was clear and rapid. First it found itself under the wing and control of France, to such a point that it moved from Rome to Avignon, at the very borders of France (1309–1377). Then came the "Great Western Schism," in which there were at the same time two popes (and sometimes even three) claiming the throne of Saint Peter (1378–1423).

In order to heal the schism, and also to reform the church, the conciliar movement came to the foreground, hoping that a council of the entire church could decide who was the true pope. Eventually, the conciliar movement was able to put an end to the schism, and all came to an agreement on a single pope. But then the council itself was divided, so that there was now one pope, but two councils. Also, soon the popes were carried away by the spirit of the Renaissance, which led them to pay more attention to the embellishment of Rome, to building beautiful palaces, and to making war with other Italian potentates, than to the spiritual life of their flock.

Like the papacy, scholastic theology—that is, theology as it was done in the universities—also found itself in crisis. On the basis of ever more subtle distinctions, and of a vocabulary ever more specialized, this theology lost contact with the daily life of Christians, and devoted significant effort to questions that were of interest only to theologians.

In response to all of this there were several reform movements, led by persons such as John Wycliff, John Huss, and Girolamo Savonarola. Others hoped that the reform of the church would come as a result of renewed studies. Still others, rather than trying to reform the church as a whole, found refuge in mysticism, which allowed them to cultivate the spiritual life and to approach God without having to deal with a church that was corrupt and apparently incapable of reformation.

Meanwhile the Byzantine Empire, ever weaker, finally succumbed to the Turkish advance.

6. Conquest and Reformation

From the Fall of Constantinople (1453) to the End of the Sixteenth Century (1600)

As indicated by the name we have given it, two important events took place during this period: (1) the "discovery" and conquest of the Americas; and (2) the Protestant Reformation.

The "discovery" and conquest are well known, although rarely mentioned as part of church history. But the fact remains that in a period of barely a hundred years Europe expanded its influence throughout much of the world, and especially in the Americas, and that one of the results was an unprecedented growth in the number of those who called themselves Christians. Thus, the conquest of the Western Hemisphere is an important part of the history of the church, and the church remains to this day greatly influenced by those events.

The date that is usually given as the beginning of the Reformation is 1517, when Luther posted his famous 95 theses. Although, as we saw in the previous section, there had been reform movements for a long time, it was with Luther and his followers that the movement for reformation gained an irresistible momentum.

However, not all those who abandoned Roman Catholicism became followers of Luther and his theology. There soon appeared another movement in Switzerland, first under the direction of Ulrich Zwingli, and then of John Calvin, which gave birth to the churches that we now call "Reformed" and "Presbyterian." Others took more radical positions, and were known by their enemies with the pejorative name of "anabaptists"—that is to say, rebaptizers. Out of this wing of the Reformation come the Mennonites and several other groups. In England there was a different sort of reformation, which while following the theology of Protestantism (and especially that of Calvin) retained its ancient traditions regarding worship and church governance. This is the Church of England, from which come the various churches that are today called "Anglican" and "Episcopal."

Partly as a response to the Protestant Reformation, and partly due to its own inner dynamics, the Roman Catholic Church also underwent a renewal which is often called "Counter-Reformation," but which is much more than a mere response to the Protestant reformation.

By the time this period came to a close, and not without much struggle and even wars, Protestantism had deep roots in Germany, England, Scotland, Scandinavia, and the Netherlands. In France, after long wars in which religion was an important factor, a compromise was reached temporarily so that, while the king was Catholic, Protestants were tolerated. In Spain, Italy, Poland, and other countries, Protestantism was stamped out by force.

7. The Seventeenth and Eighteenth Centuries

During this period the strong religious convictions of various groups—especially of Catholics and Protestants—led to bloody wars that sometimes decimated the population. Germany and much of the rest of Europe saw the Thirty Years' War (1618–1648), arguably the bloodiest that Europe had ever suffered. In France the earlier policy of tolerance was abandoned. In England the Puritan Revolution led to civil war, to the execution of King Charles the First, and to still more wars, until finally settling in a situation very similar to what existed prior to the revolution, although with more tolerance for religious dissenters than before.

All of these wars were fueled by the inflexible spirit of various orthodoxies—Roman Catholic, Lutheran, and Reformed. For each of these orthodoxies, every detail of doctrine was of the greatest importance, and therefore not even the least deviation from the most strict orthodoxy should be allowed. The result was not only the wars that have been mentioned, but also an endless series of debates among Catholics, Lutherans, and the Reformed, all of whom found it difficult to reach an agreement even within their own traditions.

One of the reactions to such strict orthodoxy and to its obviously negative consequences was the growth of rationalism. Another consequence was the emergence of a series of positions that underscored the importance of experience and obedience over orthodoxy. Among

Lutherans, pietism and the Moravian movement took this position, as did Methodism among Anglicans. Others, unhappy both with orthodoxy and with pietism, took the spiritualist option and set out to seek God, no longer in the church or the community of believers, but in the inner and private life.

Still others decided to leave Europe and settle in places where they hoped to establish a society governed by the principles they believed to be essential to the gospel—principles which sometimes included intolerance toward any who disagreed with them. Such was the origin of the British colonies in New England.

8. The Nineteenth Century

This was the great century of modernity. It began with a series of political upheavals that opened the way for the ideals of democracy and free enterprise—North American independence, the French Revolution, and then the independence of the Latin American nations. Part of the ideal of these new nations was freedom of conscience, so that no one would be forced to affirm anything of which they were not convinced. This, joined to the rationalism that had been making headway since the previous period, led many to think that only a strictly rational faith was compatible with the modern world.

Such an attitude was seen particularly among Protestant theologians, especially in Germany, but also elsewhere. This was the origin of "liberalism," a theological position that gained many followers in the nineteenth century.

While Protestantism, or at least its academic theologians and leaders, allowed itself to be swayed by the innovations of the modern world, Roman Catholicism took the opposite path. Practically anything that could be seen as modern—democracy, freedom of conscience, public schools—was considered heretical, and as such was condemned by Pope Pius IX. Also, as part of this reactionary policy, it was during this period that the pope was formally declared to be infallible (First Vatican Council, 1870).

On the other hand, while in Europe many thought that Christianity was disappearing into the past, it was precisely during this period that the Christian faith achieved such a wide geographic expansion that for the first time it became truly universal. Certainly one of the most important elements in the history of the church during the nineteenth century was its missionary expansion—especially Protestant missionary expansion—in Asia, the Pacific, Africa, the Muslim world, and Latin America.

9. The Twentieth Century and the End of Modernity

For the purposes of our division of church history into various periods, it may well be said that the nineteenth century ended with the beginning of the First World War, in 1914. Thus, this period goes from 1914 to the present.

The rationalist principles of earlier centuries, especially as applied to the sciences and to technology, brought about unexpected results. At the high point of modernity, it was believed that humankind was approaching a glorious time of abundance and joy. Every human problem would eventually be solved by means of reason and its younger sister, technology. The industrialized nations of the North Atlantic (Europe and the United States) would lead the world toward that promising future. But the twentieth century put an end to such hopes with a series of events that showed that the supposed promise of modernity was but a dream.

Throughout the world there was a rapid process of decolonization. This also was part of the end of modernity, for what actually took place was that people began to distrust the promises of modernity that had been used to justify the colonial enterprise. In Asia, Africa, and Latin America there was a strong reaction, both political and intellectual, against colonialism and neocolonialism.

In order to understand the impact of these events on the life of the church, the simplest procedure is to follow the course of the three main branches of Christianity: the Eastern, the Roman Catholic, and the Protestant.

Early in the twentieth century, the entire Eastern church was shaken by the Russian Revolution and its impact on Eastern Europe. Marxism, as applied in the Soviet Union, was a version of the promise of modernity. But toward the end of the twentieth century it was clear that the enterprise had failed and that the Russian church, which for several decades had to survive under strong governmental pressure, was showing new signs of life.

Roman Catholicism continued its struggle against various aspects of modernity throughout the first half of the twentieth century. Beginning in 1958, with the papacy of John XXIII, this particular church began to open itself to the modern world. By then, however, the world itself was rapidly moving toward postmodernity, and the theology which developed after the Second Vatican Council became increasingly critical of modernity—not on the basis of the reactionary attitude of earlier generations, but rather looking toward a future beyond modernity.

In the case of Protestantism the optimism of liberal theologians in Europe was shattered by two world wars. Something similar, although of lesser and slower impact, took place in the United States. To a degree the rebellion of Karl Barth against liberalism was a first glimpse of the need for a postmodern theology. In the United States the struggle for civil rights, and the social conflict and crises that took place late in the century, played a similar role.

On the other hand, in all Christian traditions there was also a movement parallel to anti-colonialism. The "younger" churches, which had resulted from the missionary enterprise, began claiming their autonomy and their right and obligation to interpret the gospel within their own context and from their own perspective. In Latin America, two of the most remarkable manifestations of this tendency were the growth of the Pentecostal movement and the rise of liberation theology. Throughout the world, ethnic and cultural minorities within the church, as well as women of all races, insisted on being heard.

The result was a new sort of ecumenism. Many of the roots of the ecumenical movement were in the missionary enterprise and reflection regarding it. Now, with the growth of the "younger" churches, that movement took a new turn. And the same may be said of the missionary movement itself, in which the churches that had resulted from it took an increasingly active part.

Suggested Readings

As part of the process of preparation of this "Outline," a survey was conducted among a number of college and seminary professors to discover which general surveys are most often used as textbooks in introductory courses on church history. On the basis of that survey, the "suggested readings" at the end of each chapter will refer to each of the following seven books. You may wish to select one and use it to amplify the outline given here.

Dowley, Tim, *et al.*, editors, *Introduction to the History of Christianity* (Minneapolis: Fortress, 1995).

González, Justo L., *A History of Christian Thought*, 3 vols., revised edition (Nashville: Abingdon, 1987).

González, Justo L., *The Story of Christianity*, 2 vols. (San Francisco: HarperCollins, 1984).

McManners, John, editor, *The Oxford Illustrated History of Christianity* (New York: Oxford University Press, 1993).

Marty, Martin, *A Short History of Christianity*, second edition (Minneapolis: Fortress, 1987).

Bruce L. Shelley, *Church History in Plain Language* (Waco: Word, 1982).

Walker, Williston, with Richard Norris, David Lotz, and Robert T. Handy, *A History of the Christian Church*, fourth edition (New York: Charles Scribner's Sons, 1985).

Since each of these books divides the history of Christianity in its own way, and organizes the material accordingly, the page references at the end of each of the chapters in this book will not correspond exactly with the material discussed in that chapter. This book follows most closely the order and division of the second book mentioned above, *The Story of Christianity*. Yet with very little effort the reader will be able to read any of these books in conjunction with this one.

CHAPTER 1

The Ancient Church

From the Beginnings of Christianity until Constantine Put an End to Persecution (Edict of Milan, Year 313)

This was a formative period that set the tone for the entire history of the church, for even today we live under the influence of some of the decisions made at that time.

Christianity was born in a world that already had its own religions, cultures, and social and political structures.

In order to understand the history of Christianity one must also have some understanding of the context in which it appeared, since that context was very influential in shaping Christian life and doctrine. The most immediate context of the earliest church was Judaism —first Palestinian Judaism, and then that form of Judaism which existed outside the Holy Land.

Palestinian Judaism had evolved since the writing of the last books of what we now call the Old Testament. More than three hundred years before Christ, Alexander the Great built a great empire encompassing all the territories from Greece to Egypt, and eastward as far as the very borders of India. Palestine was therefore part of that empire. One of the consequences of Alexander's conquests was "Hellenism," that is, the combination of Greek culture brought by Alexander and his followers with the ancient cultures that had long existed in each of the lands that he conquered.

Upon the death of Alexander, some of his successors retained control of Syria and Palestine. Led by the Maccabees, the Jews rebelled and managed to gain a brief period of independence, until the Romans conquered the land in 63 B.C.E. Therefore, when Jesus was born Palestine was part of the Roman Empire.

Judaism in Palestine was not all of one piece. There were within it various parties and religious groups. Chief among them were the Zealots, the Pharisees, the Sadducees, and the Essenes. These groups differed among themselves on the manner in which God was to be served, as well as on how Jews ought to relate to the Roman Empire. All agreed that there is only one God, that God's people must follow certain patterns of behavior, and that some day God's promises to that people would be fulfilled.

Beyond Palestine there were large numbers of Jews in Egypt, Asia Minor, Rome, Roman North Africa, and even the lands to the east that had earlier been ruled by Babylon. This vast Jewish contingent that spread far beyond the borders of Palestine is known as the Jewish "Diaspora," or Dispersion. In the Diaspora Judaism bore the mark of its various surrounding cultures. Within the borders of the Roman Empire this could be seen in the use of Greek—the most common language in the Hellenistic world— in preference to Hebrew or Aramaic—the common language of that part of the Diaspora which spread eastward in the direction of Babylon. Therefore it was in the Diaspora, in Egypt, that the Old Testament was translated into Greek. This translation, known as the *Septuagint,* was the Bible that most Greek-speaking Christians used for a long time. Egypt also saw the life of the Hellenistic Jewish philosopher Philo of Alexandria, who sought to combine Greek philosophy with Judaism and was therefore a forerunner of the many Christian theologians who followed a similar path regarding their Christian faith.

However, from a very early date the Christian church began to make headway beyond the limits of Judaism, to the point that it soon became mostly Gentile. In order to understand that process, it is necessary to know something regarding the political and cultural atmosphere of the times.

Politically, the entire Mediterranean basin was part of the Roman Empire, which had unified the region under its rule. In a way, that political unity contributed to the expansion of Christianity. But that unity was based on a syncretistic approach to religion, in which the mixture of various religious traditions soon became one of the most serious threats to nascent Christianity. Furthermore, part of the support for that political unity was the worship of the emperor, which soon became one of the reasons for the persecution of Christians.

Within that framework, the new faith made its way, while at the same time defining itself.

In philosophy, the ideas of Plato and his teacher Socrates were dominant. They spoke of the immortality of the soul and of an invisible and purely rational world which was far more perfect and permanent than this transient world of "appearances." Also Stoicism, a philosophical doctrine that promoted high moral values, had gained many adherents. Eventually, many Christians would come to understand the Christian doctrine of life after death in terms of the Platonic doctrine of the immortality of the soul, and the proclamation of the Reign of God as an affirmation of the Platonic world of ideas. Likewise, Stoic moral doctrine was profoundly influential in the development of Christian ethics.

The first and most important task of early Christianity was to define its own nature vis-à-vis the Jewish tradition in which it was born. As may be seen in the New Testament, a significant context for that process of definition was the mission to the Gentiles.

This story is known to us mostly through the New Testament. There we can see, particularly in the letters of Paul and in the book of Acts, the stamp of the difficult decisions the church had to make during its first decades. Would Christianity be a new sect within Judaism? Would it be open to Gentiles? How much of Judaism would Gentile converts to Christianity have to accept and follow? These were the most important and urgent questions with which the church had to struggle in its first decades of existence.

Apart from the books of the New Testament, the most ancient Christian books that have survived are usually grouped under the title of "Apostolic Fathers." It is through this collection of letters, sermons, and theological treatises that we gain most of the information available to us regarding the life and teachings of Christians after the close of the New Testament. Here we see the same process of self-definition in matters as diverse as doctrine, worship, church government, and ethics.

Soon Christianity had its first conflicts with the state, and it was within that context that the new faith had to determine its relationship with the surrounding culture, as well as with the political and social institutions that both expressed and supported that culture.

Those conflicts with the state produced both martyrs and "apologists." The first sealed their witness with their blood.

In the book of Acts, it is usually the religious leaders within Judaism that take the lead in persecuting Christians and the church. Furthermore, there are several occasions in which the imperial authorities intervene in order to quench a riot, and thus indirectly prevent the persecution of Christians.

Soon, however, things began to change, and it was the Empire that took the lead in persecuting Christians. During the first century, the worst persecutions took place under Nero (who ruled from 54 to 68) and perhaps Domitian (81–96). Although significant for the life of the church, these persecutions seem to have been relatively local, the first limited to Rome, and the second mostly to Asia Minor.

During the second century, persecution became increasingly widespread, although in general terms the policy set by Trajan (98–117) was followed. This policy consisted in punishing Christians if they were brought before the authorities and refused to recant, but at the same time not employing the resources of the state in order to seek Christians out. The result was sporadic persecution which depended mostly on local circumstances. Among the most famous martyrs of the second century are Ignatius of Antioch (from whom seven letters have survived), Polycarp of Smyrna (whose martyrdom is recorded in a fairly ancient document), Justin, and the martyrs of Lyon and Vienne, in Gaul.

During the third century, although there were long periods of relative calm, persecution became increasingly severe. Emperor Septimius Severus (193–211) followed a syncretistic policy, and decreed the death penalty for any who would convert to exclusivist religions such as Judaism or Christianity. It was during his reign that the famous martyrdom of Perpetua and Felicitas took place. Decius (249–251) ordered that all should sacrifice before the gods, and should have certificates stating that they had done so. Christians and any others who refused to sacrifice were to be treated as criminals. Valerian (253–260) followed a similar policy.

However, the worst persecution took place under Diocletian (284–305) and his immediate successors. First, Christians were expelled from the legions. Then it was ordered that their buildings and sacred books be destroyed. Finally, persecution became general, and Christians were subject, not only to death, but also to tortures of various sorts.

After the death of Diocletian, several of his successors continued his policy, until two of them, Constantine (306–337) and Licinius

(307–323) ended the persecution by the so-called "Edict of Milan" (313).

The apologists sought to defend the Christian faith in the face of the various accusations made against it. (And some, such as Justin, were first apologists and eventually martyrs.) This attempt to defend the faith produced some of the earliest theological works of Christianity.

To a large measure, persecutions were based on a number of rumors and opinions circulating among the populace regarding Christians. It was said, for instance, that they performed various acts of immorality. It was also claimed that their doctrine made no sense and was typical of people who were incapable of logical thought.

In response to that situation, the apologists wrote a series of works with the double purpose of denying the false rumors regarding Christian practice and of showing that Christianity was more than mere nonsense. Therefore, the main intellectual task of the apologists was to clarify the relationship between Christian faith and the ancient Greco-Roman culture.

Some of the apologists were openly hostile to that culture. Their defense of Christianity consisted mostly in showing that the supposedly higher culture of the Greco-Roman world was in fact not worthy of such respect. The main apologist who followed this direction was Tatian.

Others took the opposite direction. Rather than attacking pagan culture, they held that there were indeed certain values in it, but at the same time argued that these had been drawn from Christianity, or at least from Judaism. Thus, it was commonly argued that, since Moses lived long before Plato, most of the good things that Plato had to say he had learned from Moses. Yet the strongest argument, and the one that eventually had the most impact on Christian theology, was that of Justin regarding the "Logos" or Word of God. Justin was the greatest of the Christian apologists of the second century, and at the end gave witness to his faith with his death—for which reason he is known as "Justin Martyr." According to him, as the Gospel of John says, the Word or Logos of God illumines all who come to this world—including those who came before the incarnation of the Word in Jesus. Therefore, any light that anybody now has, or had in the past, is due to the same Word whom Christians know in Jesus Christ. On the basis of this argument, Justin felt free to accept whatever of value he could find in pagan culture and philosophy, and add it to his understanding of the faith. Through the course of centuries, this doctrine of the Logos as source of all truth, no matter where it may be found, has made significant impact on Christian theology, and on the manner in which many Christians have related to the surrounding culture.

But there were other challenges to faith, which most Christians eventually called "heresies"—that is, doctrines which seemed to threaten the very core of the Christian message.

The rapid growth of the church brought to it people of various religious backgrounds, and this in turn gave rise to diverse interpretations of Christianity. Although there had always been within the church a degree of theological diversity, it soon became clear that some of these various interpretations threatened what to many was the core itself of the Christian message. Such doctrines were eventually classified as "heresies."

The most important of these heresies was Gnosticism. Gnosticism was a whole conglomerate of ideas and schools that differed among themselves on many points, but which however had certain elements in common. Among those common elements were the following: First, a negative attitude toward the material world, so that "salvation" consisted in escaping from matter. Second, a notion that such salvation was attained through a special knowledge or "gnosis," through which the believer could escape from this material world and ascend to the spiritual. It is for reason of this "gnosis" that such doctrines are grouped together under the name of "Gnosticism."

Not all Gnostics were Christians. But when Christianity and Gnosticism were brought together the traditional Christian faith was threatened at several points: Gnosticism denied creation, which claims that the present physical world is God's good creation; it denied the doctrine of incarnation, which says that God took human flesh (the commonly held Gnostic doctrine, that Jesus did not have a true body such as ours, is known as "docetism"); and it denied the final resurrection, which looks forward to an eternal life in the body (although most Gnostics held that at least some souls are by nature immortal).

The other "heresy" that posed a serious challenge to Christianity during this period was the doctrine of Marcion. Like the Gnostics, Marcion denied that the good God could have created this material world. He therefore claimed that the God of the Old Testament is not the same as the Father of Jesus, but is rather an inferior being. He claimed also that while Yahweh is vengeful and cruel, the true and supreme God is loving and forgiving. In contrast to the Gnostics, who did not found churches, Marcion did found a Marcionite church. Also, since he rejected the Old Testament as the book of a lesser god, he made a list of Christian books which he said were inspired by the true God. Although Marcion's collection was much shorter than our present New Testament, it was the first such list of books of the New Testament.

It was in response to such heresies that the early church produced the canon (or list of books) of the New Testament, the creed that is usually called "the Apostles' Creed," and the doctrine of apostolic succession.

Although from a very early date the church had used the Gospels and the Letters of Paul in its worship services and catechetical instruction, what finally led to the insistence that certain Christian books were to be considered Scripture and others not was the challenge of heresies. Over against heretics who proposed their own books, or their own lists of books, the church began to determine which books were part of Christian scripture, and which not.

At the same time and for similar reasons, there appeared in Rome the "Roman symbol." This was a confession of faith that eventually evolved into what today we call "The Apostles' Creed." The purpose of that creed was clearly to reject and counteract the teachings of Gnosticism and of Marcion.

Finally, the church responded to heresy by pointing to the uninterrupted line of leaders in the main churches—lines which could be drawn back to the apostles themselves. This is the origin of the concept of apostolic succession.

All of these elements produced a church with more organization, and more clearly defined doctrines and practices. In order to distinguish the church in this period from the earlier community, historians often speak of "the ancient catholic church," and mark its beginning from the last decades of the second century.

After the apologists came the first great teachers of the faith—people such as Irenaeus, Tertullian, Clement of Alexandria, Origen, and Cyprian. They wrote works whose impact is felt to this day.

Irenaeus, Tertullian, and Clement lived late in the second century. Irenaeus was originally from Smyrna, in Asia Minor, and he spent most of his life in Lyon in what today is France. He was above all a pastor who believed that his task as a theologian consisted in strengthening his flock, especially against the threat of heresy. His theology does not claim to be original, but rather seeks to affirm what he himself learned from his teachers. This explains the recent growing interest in Irenaeus, since his writings help us to understand the earliest Christian theology.

Tertullian lived in Carthage, in North Africa. His inclination was mostly toward legal themes. He wrote in defense of the faith against pagans, and also against several heresies. He was the first to use the formula "one substance, three persons" to refer to the Trinity, and also the first to speak in terms of "one person, two substances" in Jesus Christ.

Clement of Alexandria followed the steps of Justin, seeking connections between the Christian faith and Greek philosophy. In this he was followed in turn by Origen, early in the third century. Origen was a prolific writer, much inclined to philosophical speculation. Although after his death many of his more extreme doctrines were rejected and condemned by the church, for a long time the vast majority of Greek-speaking theologians were his followers in one way or another.

Cyprian was bishop of Carthage (where Tertullian had lived before) when the persecution broke out under Decius (year 249). Cyprian fled and hid, hoping to continue leading the life of the church from his hiding place. After the persecution abated he was criticized for having fled, although he died as a martyr in a later persecution (258). For these reasons, the main matter which Cyprian debated in his writings was the question of the "lapsed," that is to say, those who had abandoned the faith in times of persecution and later wished to return to the church. Also, in part for other reasons, he clashed with the bishop of Rome. In the resulting debates, Cyprian developed his ideas regarding the nature and government of the church—ideas which are debated to this day.

At about the same time the question of the restoration of the lapsed was also debated in Rome. The most important person in that debate was Novatian, who also wrote on the Trinity.

Finally, it is important to point out that, in spite of the scarcity of documents describing it, it is possible to know something about the daily life and the worship of Christians during those first years.

Throughout this period the central act of Christian worship was communion. This was a joyous event, for it was above all a celebration of the resurrection of Jesus and a foretaste of his return. As a celebration of the resurrection, it usually took place on Sunday, the day in which the Lord had risen from the dead. Also, as a foretaste of the great heavenly banquet, communion originally involved an entire meal. Later, for various reasons, it was limited to bread and wine. Also, from an early date the custom developed of celebrating worship at the graves of martyrs and other departed Christians, in places such as the catacombs of Rome.

Baptism, the rite of initiation and grafting into the Christian community, was the other central act of worship. It usually took place on Easter Sunday, after a long period of preparation for those who were to be baptized. During the last weeks before this great event on Easter, those who were already baptized also prepared themselves for the renewal of their own baptismal vows. This is the origin of the season of Lent.

It seems that at first there were different forms of government in various churches throughout the Roman Empire, and that the titles of "elder" and "bishop" were roughly equivalent. But already toward the end of the second century the tripartite order of ministry had appeared: deacons, elders, and bishops. There were also specific ministries for women, especially within nascent monasticism.

Suggested Readings

Dowley, *Introduction to the History of Christianity*, pp. 45–128.

González, *A History of Christian Thought*, vol. 1, pp. 29–260.

González, *The Story of Christianity*, vol. 1, pp. 1–109.

McManners, *The Oxford Illustrated History of Christianity*, pp. 21–61.

Marty, *A Short History of Christianity*, pp. 15–94.

Shelley, *Church History in Plain Language*, pp. 15–102.

Walker, *A History of the Christian Church*, pp. 5–125.

CHAPTER 2

The Christian Empire

From the Edict of Milan (313) to the Fall of the Last Roman Emperor of the West (476)

With the "conversion" of the Emperor Constantine, things changed radically. The persecuted church became first the tolerated church, and eventually the official religion of the Roman Empire. In consequence the church, which until then was composed mostly of people from the lower echelons of society, made headway among the aristocracy.

The "conversion" of Constantine was a long process paralleling the route that eventually took him to absolute power over the entire Empire. Through a series of wars and maneuvers, Constantine defeated every rival and expanded his power to the point of becoming master of the Empire. Although from an early date he appears to have favored Christians, he was not baptized until he was on his death bed, and he retained the title of High Priest of the traditional pagan religion, which was one of his roles as emperor.

Although by the time Constantine died Christianity was not yet the official religion of the empire (it would not be until late in the fourth century), his policies and those of his successors left their mark in the religious life of the Roman Empire. The church, until then persecuted, now began to enjoy an ever growing prestige and power. Therefore, many now hastened to join Christianity—among them members of the aristocracy who until recently had thought that the Christian faith was most appropriate for the ignorant and the impoverished.

Constantine's conversion also left its mark on Christian worship. At the site where the ancient city of Byzantium had stood, Constantine now built Constantinople (Constantinopolis, the City of Constantine), where several churches were erected with his support and that of his successors. In Palestine and elsewhere Constantine, his mother, and then his successors did likewise. The result was that Christian worship became ever more formal, in part imitating the usage of the court. There also began to develop a typically Christian architecture, whose most common expression was the type of church known as "basilica."

The change was not easy, and Christians responded in many different ways. Some were so grateful for the new situation that it was difficult for them to take a critical stance before the government and society.

Probably this was the attitude most commonly held by the mass of Christians, although little written material expressing it has survived. Its main intellectual exponent was Eusebius of Caesarea. Eusebius had lived through the period of persecutions, and therefore the government's new attitude appeared to be a miracle to him. His most famous and influential work, the *Church History,* gives the impression that from the beginning God was preparing the way for the coming together of the church and the Empire. For Eusebius, Constantine was the "new David" who had brought about this great deed. It is through the influence of Eusebius that to this day many believe that the persecutions were mostly due to a grave misunderstanding of the church and its faith on the part of the Empire, or to the evil nature of some particularly wicked emperors.

Others fled to the desert or to remote places and took up the monastic life.

Although the origins of monasticism date from well before the time of Constantine, the new conditions impelled many to follow the monastic ideal. Now that the heroic expression of the faith of the martyrs was no longer possible, many took up the alternate heroic expression of asceticism—that is, they devoted themselves to a life of renunciation and contemplation.

The favorite places of monastic retreat were the desert in Egypt and other similar areas. It was in Egypt that Paul and Anthony lived—two hermits who are both credited by different ancient authors with having been the founders of monasticism.

Although at first monks lived alone (the very word "monk" means "solitary"), soon they began to join in groups in order to share resources and teachings. Thus developed a new form of monasticism. This new form was characterized by community life (in what today we call "monasteries") and is usually known as "cenobitic" (from Greek roots meaning "life in common"). It is said that the founder of cenobitic monasticism was Pacomius. Although there may have been other monastic communities before those founded by Pacomius, there is no doubt that he was the great organizer of cenobitic monasticism in Egypt.

Monasticism spread rapidly throughout the church. In some areas of Egypt there were tens of thousands of monks and twice as many women following the monastic way of life. Eventually the movement gained a foothold among the aristocracy in cities, where it was not unusual for a group of well-to-do women to join in a small community devoted to prayer, meditation, and study. As early as the fourth century the monastic movement was playing an important role in the theological controversies of the time—for instance, by sheltering Athanasius (one of the protagonists in the Trinitarian controversy) from his enemies. Among its main advocates were important leaders such as Jerome, who went to Bethlehem to follow the monastic way of life, and Basil the Great, who did much to organize the movement. From that point and throughout the centuries, monasticism would show an astonishing degree of flexibility, providing leadership in such diverse fields as theology, missions, agriculture, and even war (this last was particularly true at the time of the Crusades).

Still others simply broke away from the majority church, insisting that they were the true church.

This took place particularly in North Africa—in Numidia, Mauritania, and the environs of Carthage. The theological reason given for the schism was the restoration of the lapsed— that is, those who had fallen away in the hard times of persecution. The debate dealt specifically with the question of whether ministers who had lapsed during persecution still had the authority to carry forth their ministerial functions. This was important, because if the answer was that such ministers had lost all authority then people who had been baptized or ordained by unworthy ministers were not truly baptized or ordained—and the ministerial functions of people so ordained were also invalid. Although there was much debate around these issues, in truth the schism also had racial and social roots, for the population of that area was socially stratified according to ethnic origin, and the schism itself was equally stratified. Since one of the chief leaders of the schismatic group was called Donatus, the schismatics were given the name of "Donatists"—a name which obviously they did not apply to themselves.

The radical band of the Donatists, the "circumcellions," were particularly strong in the more remote areas, and became a militant group that did not hesitate to defend its cause by means of arms. Although the imperial authorities tried to suppress the circumcellions by similar means, they managed to continue at least until the Arab conquests of the seventh century. It was in response to the circumcellions, and in trying to set some guidelines for action against them, that Augustine developed his theory of the "just war," which has been quite influential throughout the centuries, and is still employed by some Christians.

There was also a pagan reaction, of people seeking to re-establish the ancient religion and its relationship with the state.

Constantine was succeeded by his three sons, Constantine II, Constantius, and Constans. It was a time of turbulence both in the church and in politics, in which murder was repeatedly employed as a political tool by emperors who called themselves Christians and defenders of the true faith. When Constantius, the last of Constantine's three sons, died, he was succeeded by his cousin Julian, usually known as "the Apostate" (although in truth he does not seem to have ever been a convinced Christian). Almost all of Julian's relatives had been killed by supporters of Constantius and his brothers, and therefore Julian had no love for the faith of his cousins.

Julian tried to restore paganism to its past glory. He did not persecute Christians, but he withdrew all the privileges that his predecessors had granted them, and took steps to ridicule Christianity. He also tried to reorganize the traditional pagan religion following the model of the Christian church. But his policies did not succeed, and after his death the reformations that he had attempted were abandoned.

The most outstanding leaders of Christianity took a middle position: they continued living in the cities and taking part of the life of society, but with a critical stance. It was thus that, finally freed from the constant threat of persecution, the church produced some of its greatest teachers. It was a time in which great theological treatises were produced, as well as important works of spirituality, and the first history of the church.

Athanasius of Alexandria was the great advocate of the decisions of the Council of Nicea (year 325; see below). This made him clash with imperial authorities who tried to undo those decisions, and the political vicissitudes of the time forced him into repeated exiles. Probably his greatest contribution was in managing to create an understanding among those who held the Nicene formula (*"homoousios,"* of the same substance) and those who preferred a different formula (*"homoiousios,"* of a similar substance) in order to reject Arianism, which Nicea had condemned. (The Arian controversy will be summarized later in this chapter.)

His work was continued by the "great Cappadocians"—a title which usually includes Basil of Caesarea, Gregory of Nyssa, and Gregory of Nazianzus. Macrina, the elder sister of Basil and Gregory of Nyssa, has not always been remembered by historians. Nonetheless, she played an important role in the life of her brothers and, through them, made an impact on the rest of the church. Basil the Great was bishop of Caesarea, among whose writings was an important treatise on the Holy Spirit. His younger brother Gregory of Nyssa was above all a mystic. Their common friend, Gregory of Nazianzus, was a famous orator. One of his most important works is *Five Theological Orations on the Trinity.* Working together, the Cappadocians continued the work of Athanasius, clarifying the doctrine of the Trinity until it was confirmed definitively by the Council of Constantinople (year 381).

Ambrose was a high government officer who was unexpectedly elected bishop of Milan. He repeatedly clashed with Empress Justina, who defended Arianism, and later with the very powerful emperor Theodosius, whose cruelty he reprimanded. His preaching was an instrument for the conversion of Augustine.

John Chrysostom ("the golden-mouthed") was one of the most famous preachers of all times. A native of Antioch, he eventually became Patriarch of Constantinople, where he attacked the injustices committed by the powerful. As a result, he died in exile.

Jerome was well versed in classical culture. He sought refuge as a monk in Palestine. His main contribution was the translation of the Bible to the Latin of his time. That translation, known as the *Vulgate,* was the Bible of the Latin West throughout the Middle Ages.

Finally, Augustine of Hippo was born and raised in North Africa. His mother, Monica, made every effort to see to it that he would become a Christian. But instead Augustine became a follower and a student of Manichaean doctrine (Manichaeism was a dualistic system of thought similar to Gnosticism), and then a neoplatonist. He finally was converted and baptized as a Christian in Milan, where he taught rhetoric. He returned to Africa, hoping to live as a monk, but shortly thereafter was made bishop of Hippo.

As a bishop, Augustine wrote against Manichaeism, Donatism, and Pelagianism. The latter was a doctrine that stressed human initiative in salvation. Against Donatism Augustine developed his doctrine of the church and his theory of the just war. Against Pelagianism he developed his doctrine of grace and predestination. Also, when some pagans began claiming that Rome had fallen to the Goths (year 410) because it had abandoned its ancient gods and become Christian, Augustine refuted that position in his vast work *The City of God*. His *Confessions*, in which he tells the story of how God led him so that he would become a Christian, has become one of the most read and influential pieces of Christian literature.

When Augustine died, in the year 430, the Vandals were besieging the city of Hippo—a sign that the ancient civilization was crumbling, and a new era was beginning.

But it was also a time of bitter theological controversies—especially the one that had to do with Arianism and Trinitarian doctrine.

We have already mentioned the controversies surrounding Donatism and Pelagianism. But no controversy was as far-reaching as the one that took place around Arianism. This controversy began in Alexandria, but soon involved the entire church.

Arius was a presbyter in Alexandria who held that the Word who became incarnate in Jesus, although pre-existing before the rest of creation, was not "God of very God," but was rather the first of all creatures. According to him, only the "Father" is eternal, while the "Son" or "Word" is not. In holding these doctrines, Arius and his supporters sought to preserve Christian monotheism and the immutability of God.

The opponents of Arianism countered that the church was right in worshiping Christ, who is true God, and that the very reason why we can call Christ our Savior is that he is God.

In response to the controversy, Constantine called a meeting of all Christian bishops. This meeting or council took place in Nicea in the year 325, and is usually known as the "First Ecumenical Council." It condemned Arianism, and issued a creed that, with some variations, is still said in many churches as the "Nicene Creed." But this did not put an end to the controversy. Many were unhappy with the decisions of Nicea, which seemed to equate the Father and the Son. Furthermore, political vicissitudes added fuel to the fire.

It was in those circumstances that theologians such as Athanasius and the Cappadocians worked seeking formulas and explanations which would serve to refute Arianism while at the same time responding to the concern that monotheism not be abandoned.

Finally, the Second Ecumenical Council (Constantinople, 381), definitively condemned Arianism and confirmed Trinitarian doctrine. (Although by then Arianism had already made headway among some of the neighboring "barbarian" peoples, and therefore later, when those people invaded the western regions of the Empire, Arianism would once again become an important issue for the rest of the church).

This period came to an end with the invasions of the "barbarians," Germanic peoples who broke into the Roman Empire and settled in its territories. In the year 410, the Goths took and sacked Rome itself. And in 476 the last Western emperor (Romulus Augustus) was deposed.

The fall of Rome in 410 C.E. is the date usually given for the end of antiquity and the beginning of the Middle Ages. Although this was probably the most dramatic episode signaling the decline of the Roman Empire, in fact that decline took several generations. Already in the late fourth century it became clear that the Roman legions were no longer capable of defending the borders against the pressure of their Germanic neighbors. The fall of Rome, dramatic as it was, was followed by ever more alarming signs of decline. By the time the last Roman emperor was finally deposed, in 476, the world hardly noticed.

Although this marked the end of the Western Roman Empire, in the East the empire continued for another thousand years. But even in the West the ideal of a Christian empire did not disappear. Repeatedly in the course of the history of the church we will see attempts to restore the Roman Empire and—even more importantly—we will also see that until very recent times church and state have continued to collaborate in ways patterned after the times of Constantine and his successors.

Suggested Readings

Dowley, *Introduction to the History of Christianity*, pp. 130–78.

González, *A History of Christian Thought*, vol. 1, p. 261 to vol. 2, p. 55.

González, *The Story of Christianity*, vol. 1, pp. 111–220.

McManners, *The Oxford Illustrated History of Christianity*, pp. 62–91.

Marty, *A Short History of Christianity*, pp. 97–103.

Shelley, *Church History in Plain Language*, pp. 103–78.

Walker, *A History of the Christian Church*, pp. 124–217.

CHAPTER 3

The Early Middle Ages

From the Fall of Romulus Augustus (476) to the Schism between East and West (1054)

Since the Roman Empire had earlier been divided into two main regions (the Western Empire, where Latin was spoken, and the Eastern, where Greek was spoken), the invasions of the "barbarians" did not affect all of Christendom in the same way. They had a much deeper impact on the Latin-speaking Western church than on the Eastern and Greek-speaking branch of Christianity.

In the Latin West (what today is Spain, France, Italy, etc.) there was a period of chaos. The Empire ceased to exist and its place was taken by a number of barbarian kingdoms.

The decline of the Roman Empire was due to many causes, both internal and external. It is clear that during the fourth and fifth centuries there was increased pressure from the Germanic peoples who lived beyond the Danube and the Rhine, and whom the Romans called "barbarians." Some of them made their way into the Empire by force of arms, while others were invited as allies or as settlers. As a result, toward the end of the fifth century both those who were invading the Empire and those who were defending it against the invaders were mostly of Germanic origin.

Several of the Germanic peoples that moved into the Empire eventually settled in a particular region of that Empire, and there they set up kingdoms which, although often declaring themselves part of the ancient Empire, were in truth independent.

The Vandals invaded Spain, and eventually crossed the Strait of Gibraltar in order to found a kingdom in north Africa. From that base of operations they attacked various parts of the Empire, including the city of Rome, which they sacked in the year 455. The Vandals were Arians, and they persecuted orthodox Christians. Their kingdom disappeared when the Byzantines (that is, the Eastern Roman Empire, whose capital was Constantinople) retook the area in 533.

The main Germanic people to settle in Spain were the Visigoths, who established their capital in Toledo. They too were Arians, and some of their kings persecuted the Orthodox or Catholic Christians. But in 589 King Recared embraced the Catholic faith. The most important theologian in the Visigothic kingdom was Isidore of Seville, a contemporary of Recared. The Visigothic kingdom disappeared when the Moors invaded Spain and defeated Roderick, the last Gothic king.

The main group to settle in Gaul was the Franks, with the result that the area is known today as "France." When they arrived, the Franks were pagan. But soon the influence of the conquered Christians was felt among them, and in 496 King Clovis was baptized as a Catholic Christian—and almost immediately so were most of his subjects. Two centuries later it was the Franks who stopped the advance of Islam into Europe at the Battle of Tours or Poitiers (732). Charlemagne, who was consecrated Roman Emperor in 800, was king of the Franks.

The Angles and the Saxons settled in the Romanized portion of Great Britain (toward the north, in what now is Scotland, the Picts and the Scots had never been conquered by the Romans). By then, Saint Patrick, a missionary from Great Britain, had attained the conversion of a good part of Ireland, which in turn became a missionary center. Therefore, some of the first Christian missionaries to the Angles and the Saxons came from Ireland. But others also came from the European continent. The most famous of them was Augustine of Canterbury, who was sent by Pope Gregory the Great (pope from 590 to 604) and who was instrumental in maintaining contacts between English Christianity and that which existed on the Continent.

Italy was invaded by several Germanic nations. The last Roman emperor was deposed in 476 by King Odoacre of the Heruli. But the Heruli were soon overcome by the Ostrogoths. Since the latter were Arian, the Catholic or Orthodox suffered under their government. It was under their rule that Boethius, the most outstanding thinker of his time, was put to death (524). Some time later (562) the Byzantines defeated the Ostrogoths and took over the region. But their rule was brief, for in 568 the Lombards (who also were Arians) invaded the land. This led the popes to request the support of the Franks, and was one of the main reasons for the alliance between the papacy and the Frankish kings.

Since these were times of pain, death, and disorder, Christian worship, instead of centering on the victory of the Lord and on his resurrection, began to be concerned more and more over death, sin, and repentance. Therefore communion, which until then had been a celebration, became a funereal service, in which one was to think more on one's own sins than on the victory of the Lord.

Much of the ancient culture disappeared, and the only institution that preserved some of it was the church. For that reason, even in the midst of chaos, the church became ever stronger and more influential, with monasticism and the papacy playing important roles in the process.

The towering figure of early Western monasticism was Saint Benedict, who founded the community of Monte Casino, and in 529 gave it a *Rule* which would set the course of Western monasticism for centuries to come. Among the basic principles of the Benedictine Rule were physical labor and vows of obedience, chastity, poverty, and stability—the last meaning that monks could not move from one monastery to another at will. Besides this, Benedict established the practice of gathering eight times a day in order to pray and read Scripture and other inspirational books. These are the traditional "hours" of prayer.

Soon Benedictine monasticism expanded throughout western Europe, and gave signs of great adaptability to diverse circumstances. Thus, monks were teachers, copyists of ancient manuscripts, druggists, agriculturists, and missionaries.

The second mainstay of the church during this period was the papacy. The title of "pope" has undergone a long evolution, and therefore it is impossible to say exactly who was the first "pope." (The word "papa" was a term both of endearment and respect, and in earlier times was applied to any bishop who deserved particular respect, such as Cyprian in Carthage or Athanasius in Alexandria. When the bishops of Rome began receiving that title, it was still being used for other bishops.) During this period of chaos the papacy provided a certain measure of stability, and as a result gained much prestige and power.

Leo the Great (pope from 440–461) intervened in the Christological controversies that were dividing the Greek-speaking church (to which we will return later in this chapter), and it was also he whom reports credited with having stopped Attila the Hun practically at the gates of Rome.

Pope Gregory the Great (590–604) was a man of outstanding administrative ability. Besides taking responsibility for the health and welfare of the population of Rome, he intervened in Spain, where he supported King Recared's efforts to bring the nation to the Catholic faith. It was he who sent Augustine to England, and who also was most instrumental in the spread of Benedictine monasticism throughout western Europe. He wrote copiously, and it was mostly through his writings that the Middle Ages read and interpreted the theology of Augustine of Hippo (the theologian who lived two centuries earlier and who should not be confused with Augustine of Canterbury). But, writing as he did in an age of little learning and much superstition, much of what he left for posterity were legends that his readers took for historical facts.

Gregory's successors collided both with the Lombards and with the Christian emperors of Constantinople, and this brought them ever closer to the Franks. Finally, in the year 800, Pope Leo III crowned Charlemagne, the king of the Franks, as Emperor. Thus, at least in theory, the ancient Western Roman Empire was once again restored, yet owing its new birth to the papacy.

Soon, however, the papacy entered a period of rapid decline. The brief renaissance that had taken place under Charlemagne and his successors was past, and the papacy once again fell prey to the ambitions of powerful Roman families. Several popes were murdered, some even apparently by their successors. Sometimes there was more that one claimant to the throne of Peter. At one point there was even a fifteen-year-old who became pope.

It was only toward the end of this period, in a movement headed by the monk Hildebrand (who as pope took the name of Gregory VII and reigned from 1073 to 1085) that the papacy once again took the lead in the efforts for reformation.

Meanwhile in the East, the Roman Empire (now called also the Byzantine Empire) continued for another thousand years. There the state was much more powerful than the church, and the former frequently imposed its will on the latter. There were also in that area important theological controversies that helped clarify Christological doctrine.

When the Germanic invasions brought chaos to the West, in the East the literature and knowledge of antiquity were still cultivated. Since there was much more theological activity in the East than in the West, it was there that several controversies took place, especially around issues of Christology and later on the place of images in Christian worship.

The Christological controversies dealt with the question of how Jesus Christ, while being one person, can also be at once divine and human. Already the Council of Constantinople (Second Ecumenical Council, year 381) had rejected Apollinaris' explanation, which claimed that the divine Word took the place of human reason, so that the humanity of Jesus was physically complete, but his mind was actually divine. Subsequently four other councils debated the Christological issue further:

(1) The Third Ecumenical Council took place in Ephesus in 431. It condemned the position of Nestorius, who was said to claim that in Christ there are two natures and two persons, one divine and one human. It was this council that affirmed that it is proper to call Mary the "bearer" or "mother" of God (*theotokos*).

(2) The Fourth Ecumenical Council met in Chalcedon (451) and condemned Monophysism— the doctrine that in Christ there is only a divine nature, for the human is absorbed into divinity. The Council affirmed that in Christ there are two natures joined in a single person. This is the doctrine held by most churches to this day.

(3) The Fifth Ecumenical Council (II Constantinople, 553) condemned the writings of three authors that some called "Nestorian"—the so called "Three chapters."

(4) The Sixth Ecumenical Council (III Constantinople, 680–681) condemned "Monothelism," according to which there is in Christ only one will, although there are two natures united in a single person.

One of the reasons for these controversies, as well as for the constant search for a formula that all could accept, was the repeated intervention of imperial authorities who wished to have all Christians agree in doctrinal questions, so that they would support imperial policy, not only in religious matters, but on other issues as well.

The final great doctrinal controversy of this period had to do with the question of images. Several emperors issued edicts against their use; but many among the people, and especially the monks, insisted on keeping them. Finally, after long debates, the Seventh Ecumenical Council (II Nicea, 787) declared that worship in the strict sense is due only to God, but that holy images or icons are worthy of veneration. Although this controversy took place mostly in the East, it was also felt in the West, where for some time there was significant opposition to the decisions of this Council.

One of the results of these controversies was a number of dissident or independent churches that continue to this day—the churches that are usually called "Nestorian" and "Monophysite."

The "Nestorians," who rejected the decisions of the Council of Ephesus, became especially strong in Persia. From there they expanded into Arabia, India, and even China. Today their strongest concentrations are in Iran, Iraq, and Syria.

The "Monophysites" gained strength in Armenia, Egypt, Ethiopia, and Syria. Armenia had become Christian even before the time of Constantine. When the Council of Chalcedon gathered, there were no Armenian representatives, mostly because the country was being invaded by the Persians. Since the Roman Empire did not come to the defense of their country, the Armenians became very distrustful of anything having to do with that Empire. Therefore their church rejected the understanding of Christianity promoted by Byzantium and became Monophysite. Since at a later time Armenians suffered persecution, they were dispersed throughout the world, and therefore today there are Armenian Christians in different regions, including the Western Hemisphere.

The Copts of Egypt, that is, the descendants of the ancient Egyptians, also rejected the decisions of Chalcedon, mostly for political and social reasons—they felt oppressed by the Greeks, who represented both the Roman authorities and Chalcedonian orthodoxy. As a result, to this day the Coptic church rejects the decisions of the Council of Chalcedon, and therefore others call it "Monophysite."

The church in Ethiopia had been founded in the fourth century by missionaries from Egypt. Since Egypt was one of the most important centers of Monophysism, the Ethiopians followed that doctrinal lead as well.

For reasons similar to those of the Copts, many Syrians took a stance comparable to that of the Copts, rejecting the Council of Chalcedon and being dubbed "Monophysites" by those who disagreed with them. Their missionary expansion eventually reached as far as India. Today they are called "Jacobites," in honor of their great missionary and organizer, Jacobus Baradaeus.

Toward the middle of this period, Islam arose as a new threat to the church. It soon conquered vast territories and cities that until then had been important centers in the life of the church—Jerusalem, Antioch, Alexandria, Carthage, etc.

Mohammed began his religious career approximately in the year 610. In 622 he fled to Medina, and Muslims count that date as the beginning of the new era. When he died ten years later, he had conquered almost all of Arabia.

His successors continued his policy of military expansion. With almost incredible speed, Islam conquered the ancient Persian Empire, thereby extending its frontiers to the very borders of India, and also conquered significant portions of the Roman Empire: Damascus (635), Antioch (637), Jerusalem (638), Alexandria (642), Carthage (695), and even Spain (711). Finally, one hundred years after the death of the Prophet, the Franks finally stopped the advance of Islam into western Europe in the battle of Tours or Poitiers (732).

These conquests had sad consequences for trade and letters in western Europe, which became even more isolated from the ancient sources of knowledge. For some time the Byzantine Empire was the main heir to the wisdom of antiquity—until the Muslim world appropriated that wisdom and carried it much further than Byzantium itself.

The result was that Christianity, which until that time had existed mainly around an axis running from east to west across the Mediterranean, now began to revolve around a new line running from north to south, from the kingdom of the Franks to Rome. However, although here in the West the church seemed to be quite powerful, the truth was that it had difficulty trying to stem the surrounding chaos—and that to a degree the strife within the church itself contributed to the chaos. The measure of order that was achieved took the form of "feudalism," in which each feudal lord followed his own policies, making war as he pleased, and sometimes even falling into brigandage.

Charlemagne and his immediate successors brought a certain measure of order and welfare to the lands under their rule. There was an awakening in studies, and a restoration of monastic life. As a consequence there was also renewed theological activity which manifested itself in a series of controversies over subjects such as predestination, the perpetual virginity of Mary, the nature of the soul, the presence of Christ in communion, etc. But this renaissance was short lived. Partly due to the advance of Islam, the European economy turned inward upon itself. Trade declined. Money practically disappeared. The only source and expression of wealth was now land. This gave rise to the feudal system, in which instead of kingdoms or other large states the land was now divided among "lords" who received it from others, and in turn distributed it among their vassals. Each lord owed allegiance to several others, and war among such feudal lords became endemic. This led to even further decline in trade, which was hampered by constant and unpredictable warfare as well as by the duties that various lords exacted on merchandise crossing their lands.

For the church it was also a bleak time. Many bishops became feudal lords, and participated in the constant and complicated intrigues and warfare just as actively as any other lord. Having thus become a political power, the church lost much of its moral and spiritual authority.

It was in the East that where there was still a certain degree of order, and where the literature and the knowledge of antiquity were best preserved. But Constantinople, the ancient capital of the Byzantine Empire, was progressively losing its influence. Probably the greatest achievement of Byzantine Christianity was the conversion of Russia, usually dated on the year 988.

As a result of the advance of Islam, the Byzantine Empire had lost all of its territories in Africa, and most in Asia. Therefore the missionaries of the Eastern church and the diplomats of the Byzantine Empire went mostly towards the north and northeast, that is, toward central Europe and Russia. Although the Byzantines sought to establish their hegemony over central Europe, in most cases those lands, on becoming Christian, chose to relate to the church of Rome rather than to that of Constantinople.

The main exceptions to this fact were Bulgaria and Russia. The conversion of Bulgaria took place toward the end of the ninth century. That of Russia was promoted by Queen Olga, who became a Christian in 950, and by her son, Vladimir, who followed on her steps.

The relation between the East and the West became increasingly tense, until the definitive rupture in 1054.

Thanks to the support of the Franks, the papacy no longer needed the Byzantine Empire, which in any case had lost most of its power. But the immediate cause of final rupture was the word *Filioque* ("and from the Son"), which the Latin West had added to the Nicene Creed, thus saying that the Holy Spirit proceeds "from the Father *and the Son*." For that reason (and several others) during the time of patriarch Photius (ninth century) there already was a schism—known in the West as "the schism of Photius." But the final break took place in the year 1054, when Cardinal Humbert, representing the Pope, declared that the Patriarch of Constantinople was a heretic, and broke communion with him as well as with the entire church that he represented.

Suggested Readings

Dowley, *Introduction to the History of Christianity.*, pp. 179–249.

González, *A History of Christian Thought*, vol. 2, pp. 56–156.

González, *The Story of Christianity*, vol. 1, pp. 221–76.

McManners, *The Oxford Illustrated History of Christianity*, pp. 92–195.

Marty, *A Short History of Christianity*, pp. 104–12.

Shelley, *Church History in Plain Language*, pp. 179–200.

Walker, *A History of the Christian Church*, pp. 218–79.

CHAPTER 4

The High Point of the Middle Ages

From the Schism between East and West (1054) to the Beginning of the Decline of the Papacy (1303)

The Western church stood in need of a radical reformation, and this came from among the ranks of monasticism.

Dissatisfaction with the state of the church, and particularly with its moral life, was quite strong in some monastic circles. Monastic reform began before the opening of this period, with the foundation of a monastery at Cluny (909). Then came the Cistercian reform, whose most remarkable figure was Bernard of Clairvaux (1090–1153). By the time of Bernard, however, the monastic ideal of reform had taken possession of many in the church, and even in the papacy.

This gave rise to a vast program of reformation whose goal was to rid the church of the abuses that had become common in the preceding centuries. Since it arose in monastic circles, this program of reformation took several of its characteristics from monasticism, especially its insistence on clerical celibacy, poverty, and obedience. For some of these reformers, the ideal was to turn the entire church (or at least its hierarchy) into a vast community patterned after a monastery. It was at this time that clerical celibacy became mandatory in the Western church.

Eventually those monastics who longed for a reformation came to take hold of the papacy, which gave rise to a series of reformist popes.

It was Leo IX (1049–1054) who initiated this reformation. It was an unrelenting program of reform, one of whose immediate results was the breach with Constantinople (1054), which marks the beginning of this period. After a series of popes, most of whom supported the reform, the movement reached its apex in the papacy of Gregory

VII (1073–1085). Gregory insisted on clerical celibacy, which gave rise to revolts and riots in several areas. He also condemned simony—the buying or selling of ecclesiastical positions.

This however led to conflict between the secular and the ecclesiastical authorities, and particularly between popes and emperors.

The worst of these conflicts took place between Gregory VII and Emperor Henry IV, and it had to do with the matter of "investitures"—that is, who had the right to appoint and to install bishops and other prelates. The conflict came to such an extreme that the Pope excommunicated the Emperor, who in turn marched on Italy with an army. In a famous confrontation in the castle of Canossa, Henry humbled himself before Gregory, who had no option but to forgive him. However, this episode did not end the conflict. The imperial troops invaded Italy, declared Gregory deposed, and had another appointed in his place. Gregory narrowly escaped from Henry's troops and died in exile.

Yet even the death of Gregory did not end the conflict. Emperor Henry IV continued his struggle with Popes Victor III and Urban II (the latter also famous for proclaiming the First Crusade). Part of that struggle was Henry's insistence on establishing another line of popes who were docile to his policies and whom he declared to be legitimate. Nor did the death of Henry IV put an end to the conflict, which continued under his son and successor, Henry V. Finally, in 1122, a settlement was reached between the two sides in the Concordat of Worms.

This was also the time of the Crusades, which began in 1095 and lasted for several centuries.

The Crusades had many different causes, religious as well as economic and political. The most obvious motivations were religious: to recover the Holy Land, and particularly the Holy Sepulcher, from the "infidel" Muslims; to go in pilgrimage to the holy places of Palestine; and to gain the remission of suffering in Purgatory that was promised the crusaders. Economically and politically the Crusades were a vast outpouring of landless peasants and equally landless nobles hoping to carve a better future in the lands to be taken from the Muslims; they also provided an outlet so that the war-loving feudal nobility could fight its battles in a distant land.

The First Crusade was proclaimed by Urban II in 1095. Its great preacher was Peter the Hermit, who led a first wave of crusaders usually known as the "popular crusade"—mostly peasants and other poverty-stricken people who packed their belongings and set out for the Holy Land with little planning or forethought. There followed several military contingents, each along its own path and with its own leaders. After many difficulties and conflicts with the emperor in Constantinople, they finally took Jerusalem in 1099. This gave rise to the Latin Kingdom of Jerusalem, which was patterned after the feudal style of western Europe and continued existing until the fall of Jerusalem in 1187.

The Second Crusade was proclaimed when the Turks took the city of Edessa in 1144. Its main preacher was Bernard of Clairvaux. Its military achievements were negligible.

The Third Crusade was launched in response to the news of the fall of Jerusalem (1187). Its main leaders were Emperor Frederick I Barbarossa, King Philip II Augustus of France, and King Richard the Lion Hearted of England. Militarily, it only achieved the conquest of Acre. But Richard did reach an agreement with Sultan Saladin which allowed Christians to go in pilgrimage to Jerusalem.

The Fourth Crusade was a disaster. Instead of attacking the Muslims, it took and sacked the Christian city of Constantinople, and established in it the Latin Empire of Constantinople (1204–1261), placing the church in the Byzantine Empire under the leadership of a Latin Patriarch of Constantinople, and thus theoretically ending the schism between East and West. This aggravated the ill feelings of Greek-speaking Christians toward the Latin West, and further weakened the Byzantine Empire (which was restored in 1261).

The Fifth Crusade (1219) attacked Egypt, but only managed to take the Port of Damietta, which was retaken by the Arabs two years later. The Sixth and Seventh were led by King Louis IX of France (Saint Louis), and had practically no results.

One of the consequences of the crusades was the development of military monastic orders. These had an impact on the piety of the time, as well as on trade and intellectual life.

And it was also the time of the Spanish "Reconquista"—the process by which the Moors were expelled from the Iberian Peninsula.

Most of the Iberian Peninsula had been under Muslim rule since 711. Cordoba became the capital of a caliphate, which ruled both over the Iberian Peninsula and over a significant portion of North Africa. But in the eleventh to the thirteenth centuries the fledgling Christian kingdoms of the north increased their power. In spite of reinforcing Muslim invasions from North Africa these Christian kingdoms continued to grow. By the end of the thirteenth century, all that remained in Moorish hands was the kingdom of Granada (which would continue until 1492).

Since Spain was one of the few places in which Western Christianity dealt directly with the philosophy and science of Muslims, it played an important role in the great theological awakening that took place in the thirteenth century. It was through Spain—and also through Sicily, which had a similar history—that the Christian West came to know the works of Aristotle, which Muslim scholars had been studying and debating for generations.

In part as a result of the Crusades, commerce flourished, and in consequence the cities also grew, for they themselves were centers of trade. Money, which had practically disappeared during the earlier period, began to circulate again. These events gave rise to a new class, the "bourgeoisie" (that is, people from the city), who lived by trade and later through the development of industry.

As a response to the new conditions, several new monastic orders arose. Most important among them were the Franciscans and Dominicans, known as mendicant orders for their practice of supporting themselves through begging. They produced a new awakening in missionary work.

The forerunner of the mendicant orders was Peter Waldo, the founder of the Waldensians, who was rejected and condemned by ecclesiastical authorities.

Saint Francis of Assisi, the son of a merchant who represented the new bourgeoisie, rebelled against the new order declaring that he had been wed to Lady Poverty. He gathered around himself a number of followers, and also founded a feminine branch of his order (the Poor Claires, so named after Saint Francis' feminine counterpart, Saint Claire). In contrast to Peter Waldo, who was rejected by ecclesiastical authorities, Francis managed to have his movement blessed by the pope (then Innocent III). Soon there were thousands of Franciscans throughout Europe.

Saint Dominic of Guzmán founded the order of the Dominicans or Order of Preachers. Although it also was based on vows of poverty, from the beginning this order was different from the Franciscans in that it centered its attention on study as a means of refuting heresy (especially, in the earliest years of the order, refuting the Albigensians in southern France).

Both orders grew rapidly. Soon there were Dominican missionaries among Jews and Muslims, and Franciscans in Ethiopia, India, and China. But the Franciscan movement lost some of its impetus in the midst of a series of controversies regarding the absolute poverty that Saint Francis had embraced, and which some now sought to mitigate.

The mendicant orders also penetrated the universities, where they became the leaders in the theology of the time—a theology called "scholastic."

"Scholasticism" derives its name from the fact that is was a theology that developed mostly in the schools, and eventually in the universities. Among its forerunners are Anselm of Canterbury, Peter Abelard, the Victorines, and Peter Lombard.

Anselm was the author of the famous "ontological argument" to prove the existence of God (an argument that holds that existence itself is implied in the very idea of God). He also produced a treatise on the doctrine of the atonement in which he tried to show why Jesus Christ had to be God-made-human in order to be able to offer satisfaction for human sin.

Peter Abelard (famous for his love for Eloise) was the author of "Sic et Non"—Yes and No—which was very influential in developing the scholastic method of opposing the opinions of various authorities.

The Victorines (that is, residents of the Abbey of Saint Victor in Paris) joined intellectual interests with mysticism and contemplation. Peter Lombard's work, the "Four Books of Sentences" eventually became the standard textbook for most scholastic theology.

Scholasticism was characterized by a method which consisted in citing authorities who apparently held contradictory positions, and then offering a solution to the difficulties posed by such apparent contradictions. It was also characterized by its method of commenting on various books, mostly from the Bible, but also the Sentences of Peter Lombard. Finally, it developed mostly in the universities, which originally were associations of scholars and students which appeared in the major cities of Europe precisely during this time.

That theology reached its high point in Bonaventure (a Franciscan) and Thomas Aquinas (a Dominican).

Soon both Dominicans and Franciscans found a place in the universities, where they made a mark by their scholarship and devotion. At this time (the thirteenth century) the impact of Aristotle was acutely felt on the entire intellectual life of western Europe. Since very ancient times, the West had taken for granted that Plato was the philosopher *par excellence*, and Western theology had proceeded on that assumption. But now, coming mostly through Spain, the philosophy of Aristotle re-entered the West. And much of it seemed to contradict a number of elements in traditional theology.

Faced by such a challenge, Western theologians took three different paths. Some accepted practically all that Aristotle seemed to affirm, even at the risk of going beyond the bounds of orthodoxy. These are the so called "Latin Averroists" (Averroes, a Muslim who had lived in Cordoba, was the great commentator of the works of Aristotle).

Others, while accepting some of the new philosophy, insisted on traditional theology, and only accepted those aspects of Aristotle's thought that were compatible with that theology. The main exponent of that position was Bonaventure—although this was the most commonly held position throughout the thirteenth century.

A few accepted the new philosophy and asked whether it was possible to reinterpret theology from a perspective that was essentially Aristotelian. The theologian and philosopher who made the greatest mark in this direction was Thomas Aquinas. His philosophical and theological positions, although at first widely resisted and even opposed by the ecclesiastical hierarchy and by other philosophers and theologians, eventually became the most widely accepted in Western Christendom.

The growth of cities also gave rise to the great cathedrals. The "Romanesque" style which had dominated ecclesiastical architecture in the earlier period now ceded its place to "Gothic," which produced the most impressive cathedrals of all times.

The "Romanesque" architecture, resulting from the evolution of the ancient basilicas, was solid and heavy. Walls were reinforced with massive buttresses, and had few windows. The roofs were vaulted, often built in the shape of a half-cylinder consisting of a series of arches, thus producing an enormous outward thrust on the walls. Since the walls had to be thick and solid, lighting was usually dull and scarce.

In contrast, Gothic architecture tried to make stone seem as light as possible. The vaults in the roof were composed of multiple pointed arches crossing each other, and resting on columns that in turn were held by flying buttresses—that is, buttresses set at some distance from the walls, and holding up the columns by means of arches. Since this meant that walls played a much less important role in the structure, there was ample space for stained-glass windows, and therefore Gothic architecture made abundant use of light and its effects. Its purpose was to point to heaven, rising to ever increasing heights—to such a point that there were cathedrals that collapsed in their attempt to reach higher than was architecturally sound.

Finally, it was also during this period that the papacy reached the height of its prestige and power, in the person of Innocent III (1198–1216). But already towards the end of this period, in the year 1303, the papacy had begun its decline.

The disorder and even schism that had plagued the papacy after its conflicts with the Empire did not cease until Innocent III was elected pope (1198–1216). At that point the Empire was going through a period of turbulence, and the pope was able to develop an international policy that eventually made him the most powerful person in Europe.

In the Empire itself, Innocent intervened by taking part in the selection of the new emperor. He also intervened in France, England, Spain, and even in such remote places as Iceland, Bulgaria, and Armenia. It was during his pontificate that the Fourth Crusade took Constantinople. Thus, at least in theory, the church in that city became subject to the Roman see.

Innocent III called that Fourth Lateran Council (1215), which promulgated the doctrine of transubstantiation and also issued rules on a number of other matters—confession, Jews, Muslims, Waldensians, the Inquisition, etc. The immediate successors of Innocent still held some of his prestige. But as early as the time of Boniface VIII (1294–1303) it was clear that the papacy, which still claimed its power in ever more extreme declarations, was again in decline.

Suggested Readings

Dowley, *Introduction to the History of Christianity*, pp. 250–323.

González, *A History of Christian Thought*, vol. 2, pp. 276–323.

González, *The Story of Christianity*, vol. 2, pp. 157–291.

McManners, *The Oxford Illustrated History of Christianity*, pp. 196–232.

Marty, *A Short History of Christianity*, pp. 112–54.

Shelley, *Church History in Plain Language*, pp. 201–32.

Walker, *A History of the Christian Church*, pp. 278–348.

CHAPTER 5

The Late Middle Ages

From the First Signs of Decline in the Papacy (1303) until the Fall of Constantinople (1453)

The growing bourgeoisie became an ally of the monarchy in each country, and this brought an end to feudalism and produced the beginning of modern nations. But nationalism itself soon became an obstacle to the unity of the church. During a significant part of this period, France and England were at war (the "Hundred Years' War"), and most of the rest of Europe also became involved in the conflict. It was also the time of the "plague," which decimated the population of Europe and produced great demographic and economic upheaval.

This period was marked by the great outbreak of the plague, which appeared in Europe in 1347 and repeatedly decimated the population. This caused great economic and political upheavals. Since they were often blamed for the plague, Jews were repeatedly persecuted. The same was true of many women who were accused of witchcraft. Religious expression often took a macabre overtone, and was almost exclusively directed towards death and the future life.

Since the rising bourgeoisie derived its wealth from trade, it had a vested interest in political stability and national union. The alliance between the bourgeoisie and the crown in various countries made it possible for monarchs to have standing armies, and this in turn led to the end of feudalism and the birth of modern nations. France and England led the way in this direction, but soon other nations followed. (Spain achieved its national union almost immediately after the end of this period, whereas the process took much longer for Germany and Italy.)

Nationalism, while spelling the end of feudalism, also marked the end of the medieval dream of a single people under one emperor and one pope (or, as was said then, "one flock under one shepherd"). Increasingly people thought of themselves as subjects of a particular kingdom or citizens of a nation.

As a consequence, the notion that the papacy was a transnational institution lost viability, and soon there were monarchs who sought to use the papacy for their own political ends. Since this was the time of the Hundred Years' War between France and England, and during most of this period the papacy was dominated by French interests, this led to a strong anti-papal sentiment in England as well as among its allies.

Eventually the Hundred Years' War involved practically the entire continent. It broke out around dynastic conflicts, but the real bone of contention was the fact that England held extensive possessions in what is now France. It was during that war that Joan of Arc played an important role, until she died at the stake in 1431. By the end of the war, almost all the lands which the English had held on the continent had become French.

The decline of the papacy was clear and rapid. First it found itself under the wing and control of France, to such a point that it moved from Rome to Avignon, at the very borders of France (1309–1377).

Although the Hundred Years' War actually began in 1337, from a much earlier date there had been tension and even harsh conflict between France and England. Pope Boniface VIII (1294–1303), who was convinced that papal authority extended to all secular rulers, tried to mediate between the rulers of these two countries, with the net result that both saw him as their enemy. In 1303, in what is usually called the "Events of Anagni," Boniface was humiliated and even physically struck by his enemies. France, whose monarchy had managed to bring its feudal nobility under control sooner than the rest of Europe, now used that power to humiliate Boniface and his successors, to the point of manipulating the popes to French advantage, all the while claiming that all of this was done in defense of the papacy.

From then on, the popes were incapable of offering much resistance to the will of the kings of France. In 1309, the papacy moved to Avignon, where it sought the protection of the French crown against the anarchy reigning in Rome, but where the popes became instruments of French policy. This period during which the popes resided in Avignon has been called the "Babylonian captivity of the church." One of most shameful episodes of the period was the trial of the Templars, members of a monastic order who were unjustly accused and punished, and whose wealth ended up mostly in French coffers. It was also during this time that the papacy developed a very thorough system of collecting funds from various parts of the church, and this in turn resulted in ever greater corruption. The mystic Saint Catherine of Siena became famous for her calls for the papacy to return to Rome. This return finally took place in 1377—an event that marked the end of the "Babylonian captivity" of the papacy in Avignon.

Then came the "Great Western Schism," in which there were at the same time two popes (and sometimes even three) claiming the throne of Saint Peter (1378–1423).

The Avignon popes had named many French cardinals. When these cardinals became discontent with the policies of the pope in Rome, they simply declared that his election was not valid, and elected another pope who was more to their liking.

Thus it happened that there were two popes at the same time, one in Rome and another in Avignon. Since upon their deaths both of these were succeeded by other pretenders, there were two parallel lines of popes, each declaring the other illegitimate. This is the "Great Western Schism" (1378–1423).

The Schism had enormous impact. All of western Europe was divided between two rival popes. Since this was the time of the "Hundred Years' War," that division reinforced and expressed the various rivalries resulting from the war. In order to defend his position, each pope had to increase his income, thus leading to further exploitation and corruption.

In order to heal the schism, and also to reform the church, the conciliar movement came to the foreground, hoping that a council of the entire church could decide who was the true pope. Eventually, the conciliar movement was able to put an end to the schism, and all came to an agreement on a single pope. But then the council itself was divided, so that there was now one pope, but two councils.

Conciliar theory based its ecclesiology on the philosophical position that is usually called "nominalism." According to this position, it is the faithful who constitute the church, and therefore it is they—or their bishops—who, gathered in a council, have final authority in all matters both doctrinal and moral.

The Council of Pisa (1409) tried to reform the church. In order to settle the Schism, it declared that both existing popes were deposed, and named a third. But since the other two rivals refused to acknowledge the legitimacy of the Council's action, the result was that now there were three popes instead of two.

The Council of Constance (1414–1418) continued the task of reformation. It eventually obtained the abdication of two of the claimants to the papacy. Upon the death of the third, a successor was named without major difficulties. This finally put an end to the Great Western Schism. It was also this council that condemned John Huss to burn as a heretic.

According to the conciliar plan, there were to be periodic meetings of the council, in order to continue the work of reformation. But the Council of Basel (1431–1449) itself split when some of its members moved to Ferrara, and then to Florence. Thus, the conciliar movement, which had finally put an end to the Great Western Schism, was itself divided.

Also, soon the popes were carried away by the spirit of the Renaissance, which led them to pay more attention to the embellishment of Rome, to building beautiful palaces, and to making war with other Italian potentates, than to the spiritual life of their flock.

The Renaissance was a movement originating mostly in Italy, one characterized by a return to the letters, arts, and philosophy of classical antiquity. Although many of its proponents were convinced Christians, the Renaissance derived much of its inspiration from ancient pagan tradition. Also, many of its leaders had a profound aversion to the ascetic quality of much of medieval Christianity, emphasizing instead the joys and even the pleasures of life, the beauty of the human body, and the capabilities of the human mind.

In political matters, the Renaissance in Italy was characterized by complicated intrigues in which each of the many independent states among which the Peninsula was divided—including the papacy—sought hegemony over the rest.

The popes of the Renaissance were in sharp contrast to the earlier popes of monastic inclinations, such as Gregory VII. Their purpose was to enjoy life and its beauty, and to turn Rome into the artistic and intellectual capital of the world—as well as the political capital of Italy. This required abundant financial resources, which in turn led to ever greater economic exploitation and corruption. Since several popes devoted their efforts to uniting the Italian Peninsula under their leadership, they became involved in constant wars and political intrigue. It was one of these popes, Leo X, who ruled in Rome at the beginning of the Protestant Reformation.

Like the papacy, scholastic theology—that is, theology as it was done in the universities—also found itself in crisis. On the basis of ever more subtle distinctions, and of a vocabulary ever more specialized, this theology lost contact with the daily life of Christians, and devoted significant effort to questions which were of interest only to theologians.

During this period, theology turned to increasingly subtle distinctions. There was also a growing gulf between faith and reason, on the grounds that God is not subject to human reason, and that therefore God's sovereign will is able to do anything, no matter how seemingly irrational. This trend continued to the point that eventually theologians seemed to be speaking of a capricious God.

The most distinguished theologian of this period was John Duns Scotus, in whom the Franciscan school of theology reached its apex, but whose distinctions were so refined that he became known as the "Subtle Doctor"—*Doctor Subtilis.*

The major theological movement of the time was the "nominalism" of William of Ockham and the conciliarists. This theology, besides providing support for the conciliar movement, insisted that God's sovereignty was such that God should not be made subject to any rational category or moral principle. It was this capricious God of the nominalists whom Luther came to know as a student of theology.

In response to all of this there were several reform movements, led by persons such as John Wycliff, John Huss, and Girolamo Savonarola.

Wycliff lived in England during the Great Western Schism. He was a profound theologian, deeply influenced by Augustine and tenaciously opposed to the reigning nominalist tendencies. In sharp contrast with those tendencies, he insisted that reason has an important role to play in theology. He was also convinced that the Bible should be translated into the language of the people. His Augustinian theology led him to proclaim that the true, invisible church is the company of all the predestined, and that the pope is at best the head of the visible church, which include many who are reprobate. He also rejected the doctrine of transubstantiation, insisting that, although the body and blood of Christ are present in the eucharist, this is not a material presence. After his death, some of his followers translated the Bible into English. A reform movement known as the "Lollards," inspired in part by his teachings, devoted themselves to preaching throughout England.

John Huss was a native of Bohemia, where the teachings of Wycliff reached the University of Prague. Like Wycliff, Huss insisted on the authority of the Bible to reform the life and teachings of the church. And, like Wycliff, he defined the church as the company of the predestined. He eventually attended the Council of Constance under the protection of a safe-conduct, but the Council decided to ignore that protection and ordered that he be burned at the stake.

After the death of Huss, his followers in Bohemia rebelled. The Catholics tried to crush them with a series of "crusades" against them. But eventually they were forced to reach a settlement, and to make a number of concessions to the Hussites.

Savonarola lived much later. He was a Dominican friar and fiery preacher who called for the reformation of the church in Florence. His concerns were moral rather than doctrinal. For some time he was practically master of Florence. But eventually his enemies gained the upper hand and had him burned as a heretic (1498).

There were also several other movements of reformation that were grounded among the lower classes and which in some cases called for a violent revolution. Among them an important movement was that of the "Beguines" and their masculine counterpart, the "Beghards," who were generally content with a life of contemplation at the margins of the established church; the "Flagellants," who had appeared as early as 1260, but who reached their highest point in the fourteenth century; the "Taborites" and other radical movements that were inspired in the reforms of Huss; and the movement begun by Hans Bohm in Germany.

Others hoped that the reform of the church would come as a result of renewed studies.

Many in the late Middle Ages became aware of the distance separating their culture and civilization from the best of antiquity. Sculptors, painters, poets, and architects attempted to return to the classical times of Greece and Rome, thus giving rise to the Renaissance. A similar movement arose among philosophers and writers, who felt that it was necessary to recover the writings and teachings of the ancients, whose ideas they believed had been often obscured by centuries of copying and recopying of manuscripts, as well as by the production and general acceptance of pseudonymous works falsely attributed to ancient authors.

These were the "humanists," who devoted themselves to the recovery of ancient letters. Many of these humanists had come to the conclusion that through the years Christianity had become too complicated and had lost its original direction. They thought that what was necessary in order to bring about its reformation was to return to the ancient sources and to the simplicity of original Christianity. The main exponent of this position was Erasmus of Rotterdam, who would flourish at the time of the Protestant Reformation, and whom many of the proponents of that reformation originally saw as an ally.

Still others, rather than trying to reform the church as a whole, found refuge in mysticism, which allowed them to cultivate the spiritual life and to approach God without having to deal with a church that was corrupt and apparently incapable of reformation.

Mysticism was widespread throughout Europe, but the center of most mystical activity was the basin of the Rhine. It was there that Meister Eckhart flourished. He was the foremost teacher of mysticism of his time, and eventually was accused of pantheism. Other outstanding mystics were John Tauler, Henry Suso, Jan van Ruysbroeck, and Gerard Groote.

Most of these mystics considered themselves faithful children of the church, and few clashed openly with established ecclesiastical authority. But the very form of their piety, which did not need the mediation of such authority, served to undermine the traditional understanding of the church, its hierarchy, and their function.

Meanwhile the Byzantine Empire, ever weaker, finally succumbed to the Turkish advance.

Although throughout this brief survey of history we are centering our attention on Western Christianity, one must not forget that throughout this time there were other churches which continued to exist in the East—the Greek church, the Russian church, the "Nestorians," and the various churches called "Monophysite." Of all these, the most numerous was the Greek church, the official religion of the Byzantine Empire.

Almost constantly assaulted by growing Turkish power, the Byzantine Empire was reduced to the point that eventually all that remained of it was the city of Constantinople. Finally, this last stronghold of Byzantine Christianity was taken by the Turks in 1453. This meant that the main Eastern church was now that of Russia, where Moscow began claiming the title of "third Rome"—meaning that both the first Rome and the second, Constantinople, had succumbed, and the position of leadership now belonged to Moscow. From that point on, the most important Eastern church would be the Russian Orthodox Church.

Another consequence of the fall of Constantinople was that many scholars fled to the West taking important ancient manuscripts with them, thus contributing to the spirit of the Renaissance and to the labors of the humanists.

Thus, at the end of this period the Christian world was ripe for the momentous changes that would take place in the sixteenth century.

Suggested Readings

Dowley, *Introduction to the History of Christianity*, pp. 324–44.

González, *A History of Christian Thought*, vol. 2, pp. 304–38.

González, *The Story of Christianity*, vol. 1, pp. 324–75.

McManners, *The Oxford Illustrated History of Christianity*, pp. 233–54.

Marty, *A Short History of Christianity*, pp. 155–203.

Shelley, *Church History in Plain Language*, pp. 233–51.

Walker, *A History of the Christian Church*, pp. 348–415.

CHAPTER 6

Conquest and Reformation

From the Fall of Constantinople (1453) to the End of the Sixteenth Century (1600)

As indicated by the name we have given it, two important events took place during this period: (1) the "discovery" and conquest of the Americas; and (2) the Protestant Reformation.

The "Discovery" and conquest are well known, although rarely mentioned as part of church history. But the fact remains that in a period of barely a hundred years Europe expanded its influence throughout much of the world, and especially in the Americas, and that one of the results was an unprecedented growth in the number of those who called themselves Christians. Thus, the conquest of the Western Hemisphere is an important part of the history of the church, and the church remains to this day greatly influenced by those events.

The conquest of the Americas began precisely at the same time in which, under Isabella and Ferdinand, Spain was becoming a European power. Immediately after Columbus's first voyage, steps were taken to organize the colonizing enterprise through a series of papal bulls. Almost as soon (1511), the protest began against the abuses that were being committed. Famous as defenders of the native inhabitants of these lands were Antonio de Montesinos and Bartolomé de las Casas. Soon the debate continued in Spain, where Francisco de Vitoria discussed and seriously questioned the various reasons adduced for the Spanish enterprise in "Indies."

The process of conquest began in the West Indies, where soon the native population was decimated, and slaves from Africa began to be imported. From there the Spanish went to Mexico (1521), where the ecclesiastical work of Juan de Zumárraga was notable, and from whence other colonizing missionary expeditions were launched.

Both from Mexico and from the West Indies there were expeditions to Panama and Central America, as well as to New Granada (Northern South America). In this last region one must mention the work of Saint Luis Beltrán among the Indians, and of Saint Peter Claver among the African slaves. The vast empire of the Incas was conquered in 1532, but there followed a confused period of civil war. Eventually the Viceroyalty of Perú was established. In "Florida" (which then reached as far as the Carolinas) the Spanish clashed first with the French and later with the British. The Viceroyalty of La Plata was the last to be organized. It was at its borders that the famous Jesuit missions of Paraguay flourished.

The church played a major role in this entire enterprise. In the series of papal bulls issued immediately after the "discovery"—and also in connection with Portuguese exploration of the African coast and the Far East—the crowns of Spain and Portugal were granted the rights and responsibilities of "Patronato Real" (Royal Patronage) over the church to be founded in the newly colonized lands. This meant, among other things, that the crown had the right to nominate bishops to be appointed to the colonies, to organize the church there as it saw fit, to authorize the presence of various monastic orders, and to manage the income and expenses of the newly founded churches. Since the crown naturally tended to name bishops and other prelates who were in agreement with its policies, the net result was that church and state worked closely together, as if the former were an arm of the latter's policies.

Since most of the conquistadors came to these lands seeking wealth, at first mostly in the form of precious metals, and later in the form of highly priced agricultural products, they needed the labor of those whom they dubbed "Indians." Therefore, rather than exterminate the native populations—as was done in places such as North America and Australia, where the colonizers went looking for land—means were sought to subdue them and force them to work for the colonizers. One such means was the "encomienda," or trusteeship, a system whereby a number of natives were "entrusted" to a settler who would take responsibility for teaching them the rudiments of the Christian faith. In exchange for such a service, the natives were to work for their trustee. Needless to say this became a thinly veiled form of slavery. Also, since Christian rules prohibited taking another's land or liberty without due cause, the "Requerimiento" was prepared. This was a document inviting the native lords to accept the Christian faith and the authority of king and pope. When they refused or did not respond positively—which they could hardly do, since the document was not read to them in their own language—this provided the excuse for war, expropriation, and subjugation to slavery. Clearly in all these matters the church lent itself to the ends of the colonial enterprise, providing theological justification for actions that were unjustifiable.

At the same time, however, the church also raised some of the most vigorous voices of dissent and protest—voices declaring that the entire enterprise was evil, or at least that it was being carried on in a most unchristian way.

At the same time that the Western Hemisphere was being subjected to European rule, there was significant European expansion in Africa, where the Portuguese settled in Congo, Angola, and Mozambique. From there they continued toward Asia, where the Jesuit missionary Saint Francis Xavier had a distinguished career. It was also the Portuguese who settled in the eastern tip of South America, thus beginning what today is Brazil.

In most of this missionary expansion the connection between mission and colonialism was clear. Missions were an arm of the colonial powers, and vice versa. Further, in most of these missionary endeavors very little effort was made to value the ancient cultures that were being overrun. Quite often the ancestral religious traditions of the conquered—and of African slaves transported to the Western Hemisphere—went underground, eventually to reappear in the form of popular Catholic piety. Thus, in many areas of what is now Latin America European Catholicism was combined with African and Native American devotional traditions. Sometimes these syncretistic cults developed with the support of the hierarchy, and sometimes without it; but in every case they subsisted for generations and even centuries.

The date that is usually given as the beginning of the Reformation is 1517, when Luther posted his famous 95 theses. Although, as we saw in the previous section, there had been reform movements for a long time, it was with Luther and his followers that the movement for reformation gained an irresistible momentum.

After a long spiritual pilgrimage, Luther finally came to the conviction that salvation is by grace, through faith. This led him to protest against the sale of indulgences, and against all the theology that undergirded it. His own theology, based on his understanding of the Word of God, soon led in directions which conflicted with traditional theology on several points. One of these was the authority of the church and its traditions vis-à-vis Scripture, which Luther held to be supreme. Another was the manner of Christ's presence in the Sacrament—although Luther agreed with traditional Roman Catholic doctrine that Christ is physically present in the Eucharist, he did not accept the doctrine of transubstantiation, which by then was accepted dogma of the church. Finally, Luther's own experience of the monastic life as an attempt to take heaven by storm led him to dissolve monasteries and convents, and to insist on the holiness of common life—that is, non-monastic life.

After the beginning of the Reformation there were long years of uncertainty. For a time, after the Diet of Worms (1521), Luther was exiled in Wartburg—where he took the opportunity to translate the New Testament into German. Then took place several important events: the Peasant revolt, the rupture between Luther on the one hand and Erasmus and the humanists on the other, and the ever increasing pressure applied by Charles V and other Catholic princes on Protestants. This led to the *Confession of Augsburg,* in which the main Protestant princes declared and expounded their faith. As the threat of war increased, the Protestant princes organized the "League of Schmalkald," with the purpose of defending themselves against Catholic aggression. After long years of political and armed conflict, the Peace of Augsburg was finally reached (1555), whereby Protestant princes were guaranteed the right to determine their own religion.

By then Luther had died (1546). His main successor, Philip Melanchthon, was more moderate than the great Reformer. This difference between the two, as well as other causes, led to a series of controversies among Lutherans, generally divided between the strict Lutherans and the more moderate "Philipists." These conflicts were finally settled by the *Formula of Concord,* in 1577.

However, not all those who abandoned Roman Catholicism became followers of Luther and his theology. There soon appeared another movement in Switzerland, first under the direction of Ulrich Zwingli, and then of John Calvin, which gave birth to the churches that we now call "Reformed" and "Presbyterian."

Zwingli, the reformer of Zurich, came from a humanist background, and reached conclusions similar to Luther's, although following a different path. His interest was primarily in returning to the original sources of Christianity, and therefore he rejected all that was not to be found in the New Testament. He was also a fiery patriot, who opposed the practice of Swiss soldiers serving abroad as mercenaries, and urged Swiss Protestants to defend their faith and freedom by military means. He died on the field of battle.

The great leader of this tradition in the next generation was John Calvin. Although a native of France, Calvin became head of the Reformation in Geneva (Switzerland). His position was much more moderate than Zwingli's, and may be seen in his great work, *Institutes of the Christian Religion.* The first edition of this book was small enough to fit into a pocket, but it eventually grew to comprise four large volumes. In them Calvin systematized Reformed theology, which soon had followers not only in Switzerland but throughout Europe.

In general, Reformed theology accepted most of the propositions that Luther had put forth, but insisted more on the process of sanctification that is the necessary result of justification. To that end, Reformed theologians declared that the Law, along with being a guide to the Jewish people, and an instrument to convict all of sin, has a "third use," namely, to guide Christians and Christian nations in their personal and corporate lives. Also, Reformed theology, much more than its Lutheran counterpart, insisted on the reformation of social and political life, and eventually led to revolutions in places such as Scotland, England, and the Netherlands.

Others took more radical positions, and were known by their enemies with the pejorative name of "anabaptists"—that is to say, rebaptizers. Out of this wing of the Reformation come the Mennonites and several other groups.

The Anabaptists followed to its ultimate conclusion the principle that the church must adjust to the practices of the New Testament. This led them to reject the manner in which the church had understood its relationship with society ever since the time of Constantine. Following the teachings of the New Testament, they refused to participate in military activities. Some eventually decided that, since the world is always disobedient, the true church will always be persecuted. Christians must live according to the guidelines of the Sermon on the Mount, no matter what the consequences might be.

Some among the Anabaptists came to the conclusion that the end was at hand, and this in turn led to ever more radical positions. Eventually some abandoned their pacifism and set about establishing the Kingdom of God by the force of arms. The most famous case was the city of Münster, where the radical Anabaptists took power, expelled the bishop, and set up a theocracy which they then declared was the "New Jerusalem." The movement grew increasingly radical, until the city was taken by the armies supporting the bishop, and the "King of the New Jerusalem" was captured.

Once these radical elements had been defeated, the pacifist elements, which had never disappeared, surfaced again, and ever since that time the Anabaptist tradition has been characterized by its pacifism.

In England there was a different sort of reformation, which while following the theology of Protestantism (and especially that of Calvin) retained its ancient traditions regarding worship and church governance. This is the Church of England, from which come the various churches that are today called "Anglican" and "Episcopal."

Although there had been movements of reform in England since the time of Wycliff, the Protestant Reformation gained a foothold in England on the occasion of the need of Henry VIII to have an heir to this throne. Since the pope would not annul his marriage to Catherine of Aragon, Henry declared himself the head of the church in his kingdom, had his own marriage annulled, and was wed again. During his reign the reforms that took place were very limited, for this was all that the king allowed.

Under Henry's son and successor Edward VI, who was too young to rule in his own right, the council of regents did move rapidly in the direction of Protestantism. But Edward died after a few years and was succeeded by his half-sister Mary Tudor.

Since Mary was a Catholic, she applied all her efforts to undo what Protestants had done during the previous reigns. Many Protestants were executed (among them the Archbishop of Canterbury, Thomas Cranmer) and many others went into exile. This earned the queen the sobriquet of "Bloody Mary."

At Mary's death, she was succeeded by her half-sister Elizabeth, who was a Protestant. During her long reign the Church of England developed deep roots. The many who returned from exile brought with them strong Calvinist convictions, and therefore Calvinism gained many adherents throughout the nation. The result was a church that, while Calvinist in its doctrine, retained every traditional practice that was not opposed to that doctrine. This was particularly true in worship and in church government. In worship, the *Book of Common Prayer* translated and slightly adapted most of the traditional rites and practices of an earlier time. In government, the Church of England retained the episcopacy, and the most notable change was that bishops and priests could now be married.

Partly as a response to the Protestant Reformation, and partly due to its own inner dynamics, the Roman Catholic Church also underwent a renewal which is often called "counter-reformation," but which is much more than a mere response to the Protestant reformation.

Much Catholic theology during this period was devoted to the refutation of Protestantism. Among theologians who took up this task one may mention John Eck, Robert Bellarmine, and Caesar Baronius. Eck was a learned man who led the first attacks against Luther and his teachings, and who forced Luther to declare himself in favor of positions which had been declared heretical. Bellarmine was a professor of controversy, and developed most of the arguments that have dominated Roman Catholic polemics against Protestantism ever since. Baronius was a church historian— arguably the first modern church historian—who used the tradition of the church to refute Protestant teachings.

The Catholic reformation also resulted in the birth of new monastic orders. Saint Teresa of Avila, with the collaboration of Saint John of the Cross, directed a reformation of the Carmelites, resulting in the foundation of the "Discalced Carmelites." The other great order established at this time was the Society of Jesus, or Jesuits as they came to be known, founded by Ignatius of Loyola. The Jesuits, organized under a strict system of discipline, soon became the right arm of the papacy in its struggle against Protestantism. They also excelled in missionary work, founding extensive missions in the Western Hemisphere, and sending numerous missionaries to the Far East. The most notable Jesuit missionary of the first generation was Saint Francis Xavier, one of Loyola's original companions, who preached the gospel as far as Japan. At a later time, the Jesuits were also the first to penetrate China—at that time strictly closed to foreign influence.

The reforming spirit progressively took hold among the Catholic hierarchy, until it reached its zenith in Pope Paul IV (1555–1559). This was mostly a moral and administrative reformation, for while it was very much interested in eliminating abuse and corruption, it tended to centralize power in the papacy and defended traditional doctrine. Among other measures, this reform movement sought to strengthen the Inquisition and issued an *Index* or list of forbidden books.

There was also an awakening of theology within Roman Catholicism which took place quite apart from the refutation of Protestantism. Most of the leaders in this theological enterprise were Dominicans or Jesuits. Among the Dominicans one should mention Thomas de Vi Cajetan, Francisco de Vitoria (to whom we have already referred) and Dominic Báñez. Among the Jesuits, besides Loyola himself, the most important theologian was Francis Suárez.

The high point of the Catholic reformation was the Council of Trent, which due to a complex series of political circumstances lasted almost eighteen years (1545–1563). It condemned various Protestant positions, reaffirmed Catholic doctrine, and took several steps toward the moral and administrative reformation of the church. Given the nature of the Protestant challenge, which questioned much of the received doctrine of the church, the Council of Trent was the first council to tackle practically every subject in Christian theology.

On the other hand, even after the Council of Trent the question of the relationship between grace and free will, which had been posed in anti-protestant polemics, remained unresolved within Catholicism. This led to debates which would become most vibrant during the next period of our history.

By the time this period came to a close, and not without much struggle and even wars, Protestantism had deep roots in Germany, England, Scotland, Scandinavia, and the Netherlands. In France, after long wars in which religion was an important factor, a compromise was temporarily reached in which, while the king was Catholic, Protestants were tolerated. In Spain, Italy, Poland, and other countries, Protestantism was stamped out by force.

We have already outlined the beginnings of Protestantism in Germany and England. In Scotland, Protestantism made headway thanks to the support of the nobility, who took it as a rallying point in their struggle against the crown. Its main theological leader was John Knox. When the conflict resulted in open rebellion, and Queen Mary Stuart had to flee the country, Protestantism attained its final victory. Since these Protestants opposed the episcopate, which they saw as a natural ally of the monarchy, they organized the church on the basis of presbyteries, and for that reason they are known as "Presbyterians."

In Scandinavia it was Lutheran Protestantism that gained the day, specially thanks to the help of rulers such as Christian III of Denmark and Gustavus Vasa of Sweden. Since the Reformation there took place under the leadership of the crown, the episcopacy was retained—often with previously Catholic bishops who had turned Lutheran.

In the Netherlands, Calvinistic Protestantism became a symbol of national identity in the rebellion against Spanish domination. When the Netherlands finally became independent, they were staunchly Calvinistic.

In France, Calvinism also gained many converts, especially among the nobility. Religious matters became entwined with the ongoing struggle among various ancient houses of nobility. The "Massacre of Saint Bartholomew's Day"—named after the saint of the day—took place in 1572, and in it thousands of "Huguenots" were killed (in France, Protestants received the pejorative name of "Huguenots," a term of uncertain origin.) There followed a prolonged civil war—sometimes called the "War of the Three Henrys"—out of which Henry IV emerged as victor and king. Henry himself had formerly been a Protestant and, although he declared himself to be Catholic before ascending to the throne, he did guarantee certain rights and freedoms to his former companions in arms, the Huguenots. These freedoms were guaranteed by granting the Huguenots the possession of a number of military strongholds. Eventually, in order to strengthen the power of the throne over the entire nation, these strongholds would be taken away from the Huguenots, but not without further bloodshed.

Finally, it is important to remember that, although the Inquisition was able to blot it out, Protestantism did make significant numbers of converts in other countries which eventually remained Catholic, especially Spain, Italy, and Poland. Many Protestants from these countries went into exile in Switzerland, Germany, Great Britain, and the Netherlands. Others remained underground for generations.

Suggested Readings

Dowley, *Introduction to the History of Christianity*, pp. 345–433.

González, *A History of Christian Thought*, vol. 3, pp. 13–247.

González, *The Story of Christianity*, **vol. 1, pp. 378–412**; vol. 2, pp. 1–125.

McManners, *The Oxford Illustrated History of Christianity*, pp. 254–66, 301–17.

Marty, *A Short History of Christianity*, pp. 204–67.

Shelley, *Church History in Plain Language*, pp. 253–326.

Walker, *A History of the Christian Church*, pp. 417–562.

(When discussing the sixteenth century, most surveys of church history do not deal with the conquest of the Western Hemisphere. In the above references, pages dealing specifically with this subject are in boldface. Other references are to the Reformation in Europe.)

CHAPTER 7

The Seventeenth and Eighteenth Centuries

During this period the strong religious convictions of various groups—especially of Catholics and Protestants—led to bloody wars which sometimes decimated the population. Germany and much of the rest of Europe saw the Thirty Years' War (1618–1648), arguably the bloodiest that Europe had ever suffered.

In spite of the Peace of Augsburg, for a long time there were conflicts and even armed encounters between Protestants and Catholics. Finally open warfare exploded in Bohemia after the episode that is known as "the defenestration of Prague" (1618). The Protestant Bohemians rebelled, and Catholic troops violently suppressed the rebellion, not only in Bohemia, but also in other lands where the rebels had allies. At that point the Danes intervened in defense of the Protestants, and after several indecisive but bloody battles an armistice was signed which left all parties dissatisfied. Shortly thereafter the Swedes invaded Germany under the able command of their king Gustavus Adolfus. He won significant victories for the Protestant side, but eventually was killed on the battlefield. Finally this Thirty Years' War ended with the Peace of Westphalia (1648), which guaranteed religious freedom, although only for Catholics, Lutherans, and Reformed.

In France the earlier policy of tolerance was abandoned.

That tolerance had been guaranteed by granting the Protestant leaders a number of military strongholds. Richelieu, the famous cardinal and minister of Louis XIII, while favoring the Protestant side in the Thirty Years' War because it weakened France's enemies, could not tolerate the existence within France itself of such strongholds. This led again to religious war, culminating in the siege of La Rochelle, the last Protestant possession.

The next king, Louis XIV, put an end to religious tolerance by the Edict of Fontainebleau (1685), forbidding Protestantism. At that point the authorities were surprised by the vast number of Huguenots who decided to leave the country rather than abandon their faith—and by the economic impact of their departure.

In spite of this, Protestantism continued to exist in France, in what was called "the church of the desert." When at a later date it was again tolerated, it would emerge as a small but mature and well-organized community.

In England the Puritan Revolution led to civil war, to the execution of King Charles the First, and to still more wars, until finally settling in a situation very similar to that which existed prior to the revolution, although with more tolerance for religious dissenters than before.

Elizabeth died without leaving a direct heir, and was succeeded by her cousin James, who was already king of Scotland. Under James and his son and successor Charles I, there was increasing dissatisfaction with the government's religious policy—both official and unofficial. The "Puritans" insisted on a church that must be purified from all that was not biblical, and gained increasing support in Parliament. (It is important to note that, although at a later time and in a different context "Puritan" has come to mean a person insisting on moral purity, that was not the emphasis of the first Puritans. What they sought was a church purified of all the "accretions" and "superstitions" of Roman Catholicism.)

The kings followed more traditional policies, and found support in the bishops, most of whom were quite submissive to the crown. During the reign of James I the tension between king and Parliament increased, to the point that his son and successor, Charles I, determined to rule without Parliament. He managed to do this for a number of years, but eventually was forced to call a meeting of Parliament in order to raise taxes. Parliament refused to grant the king the taxes he required until the church was reformed along more presbyterian lines. Eventually, the tension came to such a point that Charles ordered Parliament dissolved; but Parliament refused to disband. It called the *Assembly of Westminster,* whose *Confession* (1647) became a fundamental document for Calvinist orthodoxy, and took a number of other measures against the more traditional form of

Christianity and church government that the king supported. Finally, the conflicts between king and Parliament led to civil war, with the outcome that, Charles I, defeated by the forces of Parliament, was executed (1649).

There followed the "Protectorate" of Oliver Cromwell, who had come to the foreground during the civil war. Meanwhile, the Puritan party became divided among various groups such as Independents, Presbyterians, Sabbatarians, Levelers, etc. At Cromwell's death his son Richard could not continue his work, and finally the monarchy was restored in the person of Charles II. This in turn brought an anti-Puritan reaction, which continued during the reign of James II. Soon Protestants feared the possibility of a Catholic restoration.

Finally, the English rebelled, James II was deposed, and he was succeeded by William Orange and his wife, Mary (1688). The result of this "Glorious Revolution" was a fairly tolerant religious policy. In England there was great latitude of belief and practice, as long as one held to the *Thirty-nine Articles* that had become the trademark of Anglicanism. In Scotland the *Westminster Confession* was adopted, and Presbyterianism became the religion of the Realm.

All of these wars were fueled by the inflexible spirit of various orthodoxies—Roman Catholic, Lutheran, and Reformed. For each of these orthodoxies every detail of doctrine was of the greatest importance, and therefore not even the least deviation from the most strict orthodoxy should be allowed. The result was not only the wars that have been mentioned, but also an endless series of debates among Catholics, Lutherans, and the Reformed, all of whom found it difficult to reach an agreement even within their own traditions.

The debates among Catholics had to do with the authority of the Pope (Gallicanism, Febronianism, Josephism), and the relationship between grace and human participation in salvation (Jansenism, Quietism). Gallicanism was the insistence on the part of the French on the ancient "Gallican liberties" of the church in that nation. Many of the French bishops participated in this movement of resistance against the growing power of the papacy. Febronianism—named after Justin Febronius—held that since the church is the community of the faithful, and the bishops are their representatives, it is the episcopacy as a whole, and not the bishop of Rome—the pope—that should rule the church. Josephism was the name given to the attempt by Emperor Joseph II to govern and reform the church within his territories according to his own principles, and not according to the guidelines set by the popes and by the Council of Trent, which he considered obscurantist. Jansenism was the most powerful of all these movements. It was named after Cornelius Jansenius, who attempted to revive the most radical elements of Augustine's doctrines of free grace and predestination. Jansenism was repeatedly condemned by the Roman Catholic hierarchy but survived every condemnation. Progressively, as it clashed with established authority, it became politically radical. Quietism, on the other hand, advocated total passivity before God as the best means of devotion and Christian discipline. It too was repeatedly condemned by the Roman hierarchy.

We have already said how, immediately after the death of Luther, controversies erupted between the followers of Melanchthon ("Philipists") and the strict Lutherans. Even after the *Formula of Concord* these controversies continued. This was a time of "Protestant scholasticism," whose methodology was very similar to that of medieval scholasticism. It tried to define every detail of doctrine, and "deviations" such as those of George Calixtus and his "syncretism," were not permitted. (Calixtus, although accused of "syncretism," simply insisted that, no matter how significant and true Lutheran teachings might be, nothing was required of all Christians except what was believed in the first five centuries of the life of the church. In this manner he hoped to avoid unnecessary controversy among Christians, and to bring about a rapprochement among various Christian traditions. But this was no time for such rapprochements, and he was widely rejected by his own Lutheran tradition.)

Reformed orthodoxy, whose spirit was very similar to its Lutheran counterpart, centered its attention on predestination and grace. Its two high points were the Synod of Dort (1618–1619) and the Assembly of Westminster. The first condemned Arminianism—a doctrine which, according to the more strict Calvinists, gave too much active participation to the believer in the order of salvation, and therefore subverted the doctrine of the sovereign grace of God. The second promulgated the *Confession of Westminster*. Those who did not accept the decisions of Dort or the teachings of Westminster were declared heretical, and expelled from the ranks of the truly Reformed.

One of the reactions to such strict orthodoxy and to its obviously negative consequences was the growth of rationalism.

Although its antecedents are much earlier, it may be said that rationalism began with the work of René Descartes, and his attempt to apply mathematical principles to the quest for truth. On the European continent, Spinoza and Leibniz carried the movement forward. In Great Britain it took at first the form of Locke's empiricism, and then the form of Deism. In France it led to the work of the Encyclopedists, and eventually to the French Revolution. Towards the end of this period, thanks to its critique by Hume and then by Kant, it began to appear that "reason" was not as objective as previously thought. Nonetheless, many believed that only a Christianity that could prove itself to be eminently rational was worthy of belief.

Another consequence was the emergence of a series of positions which underscored the importance of experience and obedience over orthodoxy. Among Lutherans, Pietism and the Moravian movement took this position, as did Methodism among Anglicans.

The great leaders of Lutheran pietism were Philip Jakob Spener and August Hermann Francke. Both called for an awakening of personal piety built around small groups and spiritual discipline. The movement, bitterly attacked by orthodox Lutherans, found its greatest expression in the missionary enterprise which dealt with an aspect of Christian responsibility and vocation that the orthodox had ignored. One consequence of this situation was that the churches founded abroad quite often reflected the teachings of pietism to a degree that was not generally true in the mother churches.

The Moravians were originally a group of refugees from Moravia who settled in the lands of Count Zinzendorf. Soon they were influenced by Zinzendorf's living faith, and became known for their strong emphasis on the devotional life and their missionary zeal.

Methodism, founded by John Wesley and his brother Charles, was originally a movement within the Church of England, in which it hoped to remain. Like German pietism, it insisted on personal faith, encouraged by small groups or "classes." It eventually separated from the Church of England and became an independent church. It grew mostly among the masses that suffered the consequences of the Industrial Revolution, which hit England before the rest of Europe. Almost from its inception, it spread to what later would become the United States, where it grew quite strong—especially on the frontier.

Others, unhappy both with orthodoxy and with pietism, took the spiritualist option and set out to seek God, no longer in the church or the community of believers, but in the inner and private life.

Jacob Boehme (died in 1624) insisted that if one had the Holy Spirit no other physical means were necessary—not even the Bible.

George Fox taught about the "inner light," which he set against the supposed authority of the church. His followers became known as Quakers. The most famous among these was William Penn, the founder of Pennsylvania. In contrast to Boehme and Fox, Emmanuel Swedenborg was a man of high education, who was convinced that the revelations that he claimed to have received were the answer and culmination of his scientific knowledge and quest.

Still others decided to leave Europe and settle in places where they hoped to establish a society governed by the principles which they believed to be essential to the gospel—principles which sometimes included intolerance towards any who disagreed with them. Such was the origin of the British colonies in New England.

It was during this time that the "thirteen colonies" were founded in North America which would eventually give birth to the United States. The history of these colonies was varied, for each was founded by groups of individuals with different interests. Although from the point of view of the crown and of many entrepreneurs the settling of these colonies was an economic matter, many of those who came to them—and some of their founders—were moved by religious motivations. There were therefore colonies that were mostly Puritan, Roman Catholic, Baptist, etc. There were also immigrants from other parts of Europe, such as the German Anabaptists and others who went to the New World for religious as well as economic reasons.

The "Great Awakening" took place in the eighteenth century. This movement swept the colonies, and made a great contribution towards the sense of unity which would eventually turn them into a single nation. The most outstanding figure of this awakening was the Calvinist theologian Jonathan Edwards.

Suggested Readings

Dowley, *Introduction to the History of Christianity*, pp. 433–98.

González, *A History of Christian Thought*, vol. 3, pp. 248–346.

González, *The Story of Christianity*, vol. 2, pp. 127–231.

McManners, *The Oxford Illustrated History of Christianity*, pp. 266–99, 317–37.

Marty, *A Short History of Christianity*, pp. 271–93.

Shelley, *Church History in Plain Language*, pp. 327–70.

Walker, *A History of the Christian Church*, pp. 255–626.

CHAPTER 8

The Nineteenth Century

This was the great century of modernity. It began with a series of political upheavals which opened the way for the ideals of democracy and free enterprise—North American independence, the French Revolution, and then the independence of the Latin American nations. Part of the ideal of these new nations was freedom of conscience, so that no one would be forced to affirm anything of which they were not convinced.

The independence of the United States posed to the churches in the new nation the question of their relation with Great Britain and the churches there, and of the relationship between the various churches and the newly formed states. Eventually all American churches became independent, and the American Constitution assured the separation of church and state. As the frontier was pushed westward, first at the expense of the Native nations, and then of Mexico, the churches that grew most rapidly in the newly settled lands were Baptist and Methodist. The Second Great Awakening, similar to the first, soon developed highly emotive overtones, and set the pattern for what would from then on be known as "revivals," which became customary periodical celebrations in many churches.

Probably the greatest challenge facing the churches was the matter of slavery, which eventually led to civil war and resulted in schism in many denominations. Many of those schisms continued well into the twentieth century.

The growth of the Wesleyan tradition was manifested also in the birth of several "holiness churches," groups that underscored the Wesleyan theme of sanctification. Some of these also developed charismatic traits. In 1906 a great revival broke out in the Azusa Street Mission in Los Angeles, from which much of the modern Pentecostal movement is derived.

Soon North American Protestantism, in its various denominational manifestations, was a missionary force that made itself felt throughout the globe. As a result of this process many of the newly-founded churches in various parts of the world exhibited traits such as denominationalism and revivalism that were typical of North American Protestantism.

This was also the time in which new theological movements and biblical interpretations appeared. One such was dispensationalism, made popular through the influence of an edition of the Bible with notes written by Cyrus Scofield. Again, through the influence of North American Protestantism, this particular reading of the Bible soon became widespread in other areas of the world.

New discoveries often clashed with ancient interpretations of the faith during this period. Many came to the conclusion that the theory of evolution, as well as much of modern science, was completely incompatible with biblical revelation. The most important result of the clash was fundamentalism, which took that name by reason of the five "fundamentals" of Christian faith proclaimed by a conference at Niagara Falls in 1895.

This was also the time when several new religions with elements derived from Christianity appeared, such as the Mormons, Jehovah's Witnesses, and Christian Science.

The French Revolution was originally guided by a political ideology very similar to that of the American Revolution, but soon took a different path on religious matters. From a very early time the revolutionary movement in France showed hostility to the Christian faith, and eventually promulgated the "worship of reason," on whose altars many Christians were sacrificed. By the end of the French Revolution, and in spite of the restoration of the old monarchical order in politics, the Catholic Church in France was much weakened. As a response to those developments, and to other similar circumstances throughout Europe (including the revolutions of 1848), Roman Catholicism became increasingly conservative, and its hierarchy opposed the new ideals of liberty and democracy.

In Latin America the movement in favor of independence clashed with the Catholic hierarchy, most of whose members were faithful to the crown. After independence it was necessary to deal with the matter of whether or not the new nations had inherited the ancient rights given to the crowns of Spain and Portugal known as "Patronato Real"—Royal Patronage. The constant strife in politics between "liberals" (mostly merchants, industrialists, and other members of the new bourgeoisie) and "conservatives" (representing the interests of the old landed aristocracy) was closely related to conflicting attitudes towards the church, its hierarchy, and its ancient privileges. Slowly, and through much effort, various settlements were reached between the new states and the Catholic Church. But in spite of those settlements, there would be strong anti-clerical currents and feelings for a long time.

This, joined to the rationalism that had been making headway since the previous period, led many to think that only a strictly rational faith was compatible with the modern world.

Such an attitude was seen particularly among Protestant theologians, especially in Germany, but also elsewhere. This was the origin of "liberalism," a theological position that gained many followers in the nineteenth century.

The first important Protestant theologian to respond to the challenges of modernity by reinterpreting the faith was Friedrich Schleiermacher. According to Schleiermacher, Christian faith is not a matter of doctrines or of morality, but rather of a feeling of absolute dependence on God. On the basis of that feeling, Schleiermacher reinterpreted all the main doctrines of Christianity in such a way that they would not conflict with the modern view of reality. For that reason, he has been properly named the "father of liberalism."

Hegel's philosophy, which included an entire interpretation of religion and its history, soon became quite popular, and many were convinced that the Hegelian system was the final and best interpretation of Christian faith, and even of all reality. Such views drew the attack of the Danish theologian and philosopher Søren Kierkegaard, who held that Christianity is a matter of a radical decision, like a leap into the void. He also insisted that the radical reality, through which all other reality is experienced and interpreted, is existence. Since he insisted on "existence" over "essence" (thus opposing Hegel), he has been declared the founder of existentialism.

Others, such as F. C. Baur, Adolf von Harnack, and Albrecht Ritschl, devoted themselves to the historical study of the Bible and of Christianity. Although these studies clarified many matters regarding the Christian faith, they also cast doubts on many items that until then had been taken for granted. The result was a widening gap between the simple faith of the common believer, and the ever more sophisticated interpretations of scholars and theologians. It was as a reaction to these theological developments that fundamentalism arose, as well as other movements seeking to preserve orthodoxy in their own denominations or ecclesiastical traditions.

While Protestantism, or at least its academic theologians and leaders, allowed itself to be swayed by the innovations of the modern world, Roman Catholicism took the opposite path. Practically anything that could be seen as modern—democracy, freedom of conscience, public schools—was considered heretical, and as such was condemned by Pope Pius IX. Also, as part of this reactionary policy, it was during this period that the pope was formally declared to be infallible (First Vatican Council, 1870).

Partly as a response to the French Revolution and its attitude towards religion, the papacy took an openly anti-modern stance. Those theologians who sought to interpret the Catholic faith in terms of modernity were condemned and excommunicated.

This attitude reached its high point during the papacy of Pius IX (1846–1878), who promulgated the dogma of the immaculate conception of Mary (1854). Some years later, he published a "Syllabus of Errors" in which he condemned many of the modern ideals of democracy, freedom of thought, and religious liberty. Finally, in 1870, still under the leadership of the same pope, the First Vatican Council promulgated the dogma of papal infallibility. (Significantly, this last event coincided with the papacy's loss of Rome to the Italian Republic, and thus with the end of the temporal power of the popes—except for the small, theoretically independent Vatican City.)

The next pope, Leo XIII, showed himself to be relatively more progressive in matters having to do with labor relations—although he insisted that all labor unions must be Catholic. In almost all other matters he followed the conservative line of Pius IX.

The same is generally true of all the popes of the first half of the twentieth century, and hence one can say that in the Catholic church the nineteenth century continued until the death of Pius XII (1958).

On the other hand, while in Europe many thought that Christianity was disappearing into the past, it was precisely during this period that the Christian faith achieved such a wide geographic expansion that for the first time it became truly universal. Certainly one of the most important elements in the history of the church during the nineteenth century was its missionary expansion—especially Protestant missionary expansion—in Asia, the Pacific, Africa, the Muslim world, and Latin America.

The nineteenth century was the great century of European colonialism, as well as the great century of Protestant missions. The growth and success of colonialism were due to a series of political, economic, technological and other circumstances. But that very colonial success led to an awakening in missionary interest and enterprise—with the result that quite often the younger churches represented not only the faith, but also the political and economic interests of the nations from which missionaries had come to them.

In Asia it was India that drew the interest of the first missionaries, and in particular of William Carey, the first great modern advocate of missions. Not only did he set the tone for much of the missionary movement of the nineteenth century, but he also was a forerunner of the ecumenical movement, calling for collaboration among various missionary enterprises long before most church leaders were ready to heed such a call. In Southeast Asia, Adinoram Judson became equally famous. In China, after several failures and partial successes, missionaries were able to enter the mainland thanks to the infamous Opium War (1839–1842), in which Great Britain went to war with China in order to defend the opium trade, with the result that China had to make vast commercial concessions, first to Great Britain, and then to other Western powers. Soon there were thousands of missionaries in China, and eventually there was even a Chinese revolutionary movement of Christian inspiration that for a time succeeded in gaining hold of significant portions of that land. Missions in Japan followed a similar course. Japan did not allow the entry of foreigners until an American squadron forced the country to change its policies. Missionaries made use of this "open door" in order to enter the country.

In the islands of the Pacific, the voyages of Captain Cook opened the way for trade as well as for missions. Christianity was well received by many of the inhabitants of the Pacific, who soon became missionaries to neighboring islands.

Africa, hardly explored by Europeans at the beginning of the nineteenth century, had by the year 1900 been partitioned among several European powers. Here again, colonialism and mission went hand-in-hand, with missionaries often promoting colonialism in order to bring to Africa what they saw as the advantages of modernity, and colonial interests making use of missionaries to further their own ends. This may be seen in the life and work of the most famous missionary in Africa, David Livingstone, who worked on the southern regions of the continent. While devoted to preaching the gospel, Livingstone was also convinced that the introduction of modern trade would spell the end of the slave trade, and thus on occasion went to Africa as an agent of the British government and its expansionist interests.

Although the Muslim world was also colonized by European powers, missionary work there was not as successful as elsewhere. Since in many of the Muslim lands there were already ancient churches in existence, much of the missionary enterprise was devoted to attempts to reform and modernize those churches. Probably the most significant result was a number of schisms that appeared in several of the ancient churches, in which some accepted the innovations proposed by the missionaries, while most rejected them.

The nineteenth century was also the time of the first great penetration of Protestantism into Latin America. Frequently supported by liberal political leaders who wished to restrain the power of the Catholic Church and its conservative allies, Protestantism developed roots in every country of Latin America. Much of the earliest Protestant growth was due to the immigration of settlers from Scotland, England, Germany, and other European countries, invited to settle in the newly independent countries by governments seeking to weaken traditional ties with Spain and Portugal, and to strengthen ideals of democracy and freedom. The first Protestant missionaries were mostly English and Scottish, but there soon was a growing number from North America. By the end of the century, in most of the nations of Latin America there were Protestant churches built on relatively solid foundations.

Suggested Readings

Dowley, *Introduction to the History of Christianity*, pp. 499–568.

González, *A History of Christian Thought*, vol. 3, pp. 347–427.

González, *The Story of Christianity*, vol. 2, pp. 233–324.

McManners, *The Oxford Illustrated History of Christianity*, pp. 338–549.

Marty, *A Short History of Christianity*, pp. 294–335.

Shelley, *Church History in Plain Language*, pp. 371–436.

Walker, *A History of the Christian Church*, pp. 627–709.

CHAPTER 9

The Twentieth Century and the End of Modernity

For the purposes of our division of church history into various periods, it may well be said that the nineteenth century ended with the beginning of the First World War, in 1914. Thus, this period goes from 1914 to the present.

The rationalist principles of earlier centuries, especially as applied to the sciences and to technology, brought about unexpected results. At the high point of modernity, it was believed that humankind was approaching a glorious time of abundance and joy. Every human problem would eventually be solved by means of reason and its younger sister, technology. The industrialized nations of the North Atlantic (Europe and the United States) would lead the world toward that promising future.

But the twentieth century put an end to such hopes with a series of events which showed that the supposed promise of modernity was but a dream.

Although today we look at colonialism in a different light, the fact is that throughout the nineteenth century and a good part of the twentieth the colonizing powers sought to justify their enterprise on moral and religious grounds. It was thought that science, technology, and progress in general were the great contribution that the West was to make to the rest of the world. Therefore, it was "the white man's burden" to take these benefits to the more "backward" peoples of the world, and even to do this by force if it were necessary. (In the United States, the doctrine of the nation's "manifest destiny" often played a similar role to "the white man's burden.") Thus, while the colonizing powers and their entrepreneurs became rich on the basis of colonial and neocolonial systems, it was claimed that this was justified in that eventually all humanity would benefit from the progress brought about by the colonizers. However, during the twentieth century an entire series of events showed that, although the benefits of modern technology were important, they could also cost dearly. During the thirty years between 1914 and 1944 practically all of humankind became involved in two "world wars" which, although truly worldwide in their impact, were mostly due to conflicts among Western powers. In those wars, the use of modern technology produced greater casualties—and specially greater civilian casualties—than any war in the past. In Russia, and then in several dozen countries, power went to communism with its promise of a better life for all and especially for the poor and the oppressed. But, after more than seven decades of social experimentation and four of "cold war," it became clear that this other version of the modern promise was equally incapable of delivering on its claims.

Although on a smaller scale, but with equally tragic consequences, several of the poorer nations of the world became involved in civil wars in which the "advances" of technology had ample opportunity to show their deadly efficiency.

Furthermore, even in their more pacific uses, modern technological advances produced drastic ecological imbalances in every continent. In a few decades entire forests that had stood for millennia disappeared, great rivers became chemical sewers incapable of sustaining life, and in some of the most populated areas even breathing became dangerous. All of this gave rise to the growing suspicion that the globe was incapable of sustaining the sort of human life that modernity had enthusiastically promised and promoted.

Throughout the world there was a rapid process of decolonization. This also was part of the end of modernity, for what actually took place was that people began to distrust the promises of modernity which had been used to justify the colonial enterprise. In Asia, Africa, and Latin America there was a strong reaction, both political and intellectual, against colonialism and neocolonialism.

At the beginning of the twentieth century, practically the entire African continent was under European rule. By the end of that century, the map of Africa had changed radically, with the independence of dozens of new nations. Something similar took place in Asia, the Pacific, and the Caribbean. In Latin America, most of which had been politically independent since the previous century, there were ever louder voices of protest against economic neocolonialism.

Throughout the world there was a movement of return to ancient traditions, customs, and cultures that had previously been submerged and even suppressed under the impact of colonialism—thus posing to the churches the need to cope with religions and traditions that had previously seemed dead or impotent.

In order to understand the impact of these events on the life of the church, the simplest procedure is to follow the course of the three main branches of Christianity: the Eastern, the Roman Catholic, and the Protestant.

Early in the twentieth century, the entire Eastern church was shaken by the Russian Revolution and its impact on Eastern Europe. Marxism, as applied in the Soviet Union, was a version of the promise of modernity. But towards the end of the twentieth century it was clear that the enterprise had failed and that the Russian church, which for several decades had to survive under strong governmental pressure, was showing new signs of life.

The dismembering of the Ottoman Empire in the nineteenth and twentieth centuries gave rise to several national churches independent of Constantinople in countries such as Greece, Serbia, Bulgaria, and Rumania. Throughout most of the twentieth century, several of these churches lived under hostile governments (first Muslim, and then Communist). But in spite of this, they gave signs of vitality.

The Russian Church and the other Eastern churches in the various lands of the Soviet Union suffered strong pressure from the government. Many thought that these churches would disappear —partly as a result of the duress under which they lived, and partly out of their refusal to adapt to the demands of modernity. But the fact is that they outlasted the communist regimes, and that they came out of that period of trial giving signs of strength and vitality. This was due in great measure to the liturgical and catechetical traditions of orthodoxy, which many in the West did not appreciate, but which in spite of that showed themselves capable of strengthening and sustaining faith even in such difficult circumstances.

Roman Catholicism continued its struggle against various aspects of modernity throughout the first half of the twentieth century. Beginning in 1958 with the papacy of John XXIII, this particular church began to open itself to the modern world. By then, however, the world itself was rapidly moving toward postmodernity, and the theology which developed after the Second Vatican Council became increasingly critical of modernity—not on the basis of the reactionary attitude of earlier generations, but rather looking toward a future beyond modernity.

The popes of the first half of the twentieth century continued the policies of their predecessors. For them what was important was to defend the church and its privileges at any price. Therefore several of them showed sympathy towards fascism, and none took a heroic stance before the challenges and tragedies of the first half of the twentieth century. Several of the most outspoken defenders of more open theological positions were silenced by the Vatican.

This attitude changed with the election of John XXIII, who saw the need to open the church to the contemporary world and to respond to the real needs of the people. That was the main reason why he called the Second Vatican Council. In that Council most of the bishops represented churches from the Third World, mostly poor. Several of the theologians who had been silenced by earlier popes attended the Council as "periti" (experts). Therefore, the Council declared its solidarity with "the joys and hopes, the pains and anguish" of the contemporary world, and took measures favoring freedom of conscience, the development of liturgies fitting each culture and condition, the celebration of the mass in the vernacular language of each land, etc.

Although since the death of John XXIII some of that impulse has been lost, the forces that were unleashed cannot be contained, and therefore the Roman Catholic Church has faced the postmodern future with new vitality, but also suffering from strong inner dissensions.

In the case of Protestantism the optimism of liberal theologians in Europe was shattered by two world wars. Something similar, although of lesser and slower impact, took place in the United States. To a degree the rebellion of Karl Barth against liberalism was a first glimpse of the need for a postmodern theology. In the United States, the struggle for civil rights, and the social conflict and crises that took place late in the century, played a similar role.

During the first half of the twentieth century Europe continued to be the main center of Protestant theological activity. Most outstanding among the theologians of this period was Karl Barth, who reacted against the liberalism of his teachers with a "theology of the Word of God," "theology of crisis," or "neo-orthodoxy." Although few followed him in every detail of his teachings, Barth's impact was enormous and he may well be said to mark the end of liberalism.

It was on the basis of this new theology that some branches of German Protestantism were able to meet the challenges of Nazism, especially in the famous "Barmen Declaration." That theology was also the inspiration of the best known martyr of the time, Dietrich Bonhoeffer.

Much theological activity in Europe was devoted to the dialogue with Marxism—especially with certain thinkers whom other Marxists did not consider orthodox. The best known theologian working at this task was the Czech Joseph Hromádka.

At the same time, the process of secularization that was typical of the modern age continued in Western Europe, where the number of those actively participating in the life of the church did not stop its decline.

Events in the United States followed a similar, albeit less dramatic, path. There the Niebuhr brothers (H. Richard and Reinhold) played a role similar to that of Barth in Europe. The struggle for the civil rights of African Americans, under the leadership of Martin Luther King, Jr., offered opportunities for radical obedience—that is, obedience to God and disobedience to unjust human laws—similar to those provided by Nazism in Europe. Also in the United States, although to a lesser degree than in much of Western Europe, the process of secularization was evident.

On the other hand, in all Christian traditions there was also a movement parallel to anti-colonialism. The "younger" churches, which had resulted from the missionary enterprise, began claiming their autonomy and their right and obligation to interpret the gospel within their own context and from their own perspective. In Latin America, one of the most remarkable manifestations of this tendency was the growth of the Pentecostal movement. Throughout the world, ethnic and cultural minorities within the church, as well as women of all races, insisted on being heard.

In Asia, Africa, and Latin America new theological currents appeared that took into account the political, economic, and cultural circumstances of each place. Throughout the Christian world ethnic minorities as well as women began claiming that traditional theologies did not respond to their condition nor their experiences. This gave rise to a number of theologies jointly known as "contextual theologies"—for instance, Latin American liberation theology, the various feminist theologies, Black theology in the United States and elsewhere, etc.—although the truth is that all theology has always been contextual. In several of their manifestations these various theologies have enriched theological dialogue and have called the church to acknowledge dimensions in the gospel that have been often ignored or forgotten. To a certain degree the development of these theologies is a sign of the end of modernity, which took for granted that the manner of thinking and acting of the intellectual elites of the West would eventually be accepted throughout the world.

Something similar has happened with the Pentecostal movement. That movement, in its many manifestations, has made enormous headway throughout the world, and particularly in Latin America. Although during its early stages it was suspicious of theological reflection and inquiry, toward the end of the twentieth century it already had a number of distinguished theologians, and was beginning to make an impact on the rest of Christian theology. This too was a sign of the end of modernity, for at the high tide of modernity it was thought that belief in miracles, in the experience of the presence of the Holy Spirit, and in gifts such as speaking in tongues and the like were a matter of past ignorance. Today, when modernity gives signs of failing, one of those signs is precisely the growth and impact of Pentecostalism.

The result was a new sort of ecumenism. Many of the roots of the ecumenical movement were in the missionary enterprise and reflection regarding it. Now, with the growth of the "younger" churches, that movement took a new turn. And the same may be said of the missionary movement itself, in which the churches that had resulted from it took an increasingly active part.

The modern ecumenical movement was born of many strands, but particularly out of the missionary movement, since those who served in distant lands soon became aware that divisions among Christians were one of the main obstacles to the conversion of others. As a result several missionary conferences gathered seeking greater collaboration and communication among the various missionary enterprises. The most important of these conferences took place in Edinburgh, Scotland, in 1910. That conference stands at the root of the International Missionary Council, the Faith and Order movement, and eventually the World Council of Churches. For a long time these organizations and others like them were the main expression of the quest for unity among Christians.

However, with the growth of the younger churches, and especially of indigenous churches that do not derive their existence directly from Western missions, that situation has changed. At the same time that the World Council of Churches and other similar agencies seek to express Christian unity, in each country and place in the world there are other expressions of unity and collaboration among Christians. In several countries a number of the so-called younger churches have united as one, thus showing greater flexibility and creativity than their own mother churches. In other places missionary societies and public service organizations have developed which depend exclusively on local resources, without any dependence on foreign funds or support.

But most remarkable, and what truly marks the beginning of a new age in the history of the church, is the change that has taken place in the demographic composition and the geographic distribution of Christianity. "While, in 1900, 49.9 percent of all Christians lived in Europe, by 1985 that number is estimated to be 27.2 percent. And, while in 1900, 81.1 percent of all Christians were white, projections are that by the year 2000 that number will be reduced to 39.8 percent. Therefore, no matter how one reacts to the various emerging theologies of the Third World, it seems likely that the twenty-first century will be marked by a vast missionary enterprise from the South to the North. Thus, the lands that a century before were considered 'ends of the earth' will have an opportunity to witness to the descendants of those who had earlier witnessed to them."*

Suggested Readings

Dowley, *Introduction to the History of Christianity*, pp. 569–640.

González, *A History of Christian Thought*, vol. 3, pp. 428–76.

González, *The Story of Christianity*, vol. 2, pp. 325–98.

McManners, *The Oxford Illustrated History of Christianity*, pp. 551–665.

Marty, *A Short History of Christianity, pp. 336–54.*

Shelley, *Church History in Plain Language*, pp. 437–95.

*González, *The Story of Christianity*, 2:396-97.

Made in the USA
Monee, IL
07 February 2024

53123170R00056